family
handyman

HANDY
HINTS

Text, photography and illustrations for *Family Handyman Handy Hints* are based on articles previously published in *Family Handyman* magazine (2915 Commers Dr., Suite 700, Eagan, MN 55121, familyhandyman.com). For information on advertising in Family Handyman magazine, call 646-518-4215.

**PHOTOGRAPHY CREDITS**
**Reader-Supplied Images: 12** Galen Lesher; **16** Walter Koldanus;
**46** Philip Saba; **55** Donnie Dressler; **59** Cameron Lidestri;
**67** *t* Lori Bosiger; **92** *t* Ann Flanery; **94** Corleen Nowicki;
**95** Judi Collins; **110** Mike Barnes; **118** Roy Edwards;
**119, 156** Craig Bingman; **134** Harold Niekamp;
**144** David Gugliuzza; **158** *t* Robert Slunaker; **208** *t* Greg Flesher
**Getty Images: Chapter openers/hexagon pattern** carduus; **31** Tek Image/Science
Photo Library; **80** My Photos for Your Work and Joy!
**Shutterstock: 193** Clare Louise Jackson; **194** *b* Gladskikh Tatiana

All other photographs by Tom Fenenga, Mike Krivit and Bill Zuehlke

Dated ISBN: 978-1-62145-587-5
Undated ISBN: 978-1-62145-588-2
Dated component number: 119100100H
Undated component number: 119100102H
LOCC: 2021938423

**A NOTE TO OUR READERS**
All do-it-yourself activities involve a degree of risk. Skills, materials, tools and site conditions vary widely. Although the editors have made every effort to ensure accuracy, the reader remains responsible for the selection and use of tools, materials and methods. Always obey local codes and laws, follow manufacturer instructions and observe safety precautions.

PRINTED IN THE UNITED STATES OF AMERICA
1 3 5 7 9 10 8 6 4 2

# SAFETY FIRST—ALWAYS!

Tackling home improvement projects and repairs can be endlessly rewarding. But as most of us know, with the rewards come risks. DIYers use chain saws, climb ladders and tear into walls that can contain big and hazardous surprises.

The good news is, armed with the right knowledge, tools and procedures, homeowners can minimize risk. As you go about your projects and repairs, stay alert for these hazards:

## ALUMINUM WIRING

Aluminum wiring, installed in about 7 million homes between 1965 and 1973, requires special techniques and materials to make safe connections. This wiring is dull gray, not the dull orange characteristic of copper. Hire a licensed electrician certified to work with it. For more information, go to *cpsc.gov* and search for aluminum wiring."

## SPONTANEOUS COMBUSTION

Rags saturated with oil finishes like Danish oil and linseed oil, and oil-based paints and stains can spontaneously combust if left bunched up. Always dry them outdoors, spread out loosely. When the oil has thoroughly dried, you can safely throw them in the trash.

## VISION AND HEARING PROTECTION

Safety glasses or goggles should be worn whenever you're working on DIY projects that involve chemicals, dust and anything that could shatter or chip off and hit your eye. Sounds louder than 80 decibels (dB) are considered potentially dangerous. Sound levels from a lawn mower can be 90 dB, and shop tools and chain saws can be 90 to 100 dB.

## LEAD PAINT

If your home was built before 1979, it may contain lead paint, which is a serious health hazard, especially for children age 6 and under. Take precautions when you scrape or remove it. Contact your public health department for detailed safety information or call 800-424-LEAD (5323) to receive an information pamphlet. Or visit *epa.gov/lead*.

## BURIED UTILITIES

A few days before you dig in your yard, have your underground water, gas and electrical lines marked. Just call 811 or go to call811.com.

## SMOKE AND CARBON MONOXIDE (CO) ALARMS

The risk of dying in reported home structure fires is cut in half in homes with working smoke alarms. Test your smoke alarms every month, replace batteries as necessary and replace units that are more than 10 years old. As you make your home more energy-efficient and airtight, existing ducts and chimneys can't always successfully vent combustion gases, including potentially deadly carbon monoxide (CO). Install a UL-listed CO detector, and test your CO and smoke alarms at the same time.

## FIVE-GALLON BUCKETS AND WINDOW COVERING CORDS

Anywhere from 10 to 40 children a year drown in 5-gallon buckets, according to the U.S. Consumer Products Safety Commission. Always store them upside down and store those containing liquid with the covers securely snapped.

According to Parents for Window Blind Safety, hundreds of children in the United States are injured every year after becoming entangled in looped window treatment cords. For more information, visit *pfwbs.org*.

## WORKING UP HIGH

If you have to get up on your roof to do a repair or installation, always install roof brackets and wear a roof harness.

## ASBESTOS

Texture sprayed on ceilings before 1978, adhesives and tiles for vinyl and asphalt floors before 1980, and vermiculite insulation (with gray granules) all may contain asbestos. Other building materials, made between 1940 and 1980, could also contain asbestos. If you suspect that materials you're removing or working around contain asbestos, contact your health department or visit *epa.gov/asbestos* for information.

**FOR ADDITIONAL INFORMATION ABOUT HOME SAFETY, VISIT HOMESAFETYCOUNCIL.ORG. THIS SITE OFFERS HELPFUL INFORMATION ABOUT DOZENS OF HOME SAFETY ISSUES.**

# CONTENTS

# CHAPTER 1

# CLEANING

# Tarp Trailer

With a big plastic tarp, you can easily drag leaves, branches or mulch around your yard to wherever you need it. A 9 x 12-ft. tarp costs around $9 at home centers and hardware stores.

## BLISTER BUSTER

Try raking leaves as if you're sweeping the floor with a broom. If you just keep your thumb and fingers on the same side of the pole, you get just as much gripping power—without the blisters!

# HARDER-WORKING WHEELBARROW

You can use your wheelbarrow for hauling yard waste, tree limbs, tools and lumber. To keep the tree limbs contained and the lumber balanced, stretch bungee cords across the top of the load and hook them under the lip of the wheelbarrow. If yours doesn't have a big enough lip, drill a couple of holes in the top edge on each side of the wheelbarrow and hook the bungee cords through the holes.

Join the Club
GARDEN CLUB
homedepot.com/gardenclub
Membership is FREE and includes exclusive offers, expert advice and more.

TIPS FOR A HEALTHY LAWN

FERTILIZE REGULARLY

MOW TALL

CONTROL WEEDS

WATER DEEP

# Leaf Bag Stiffener

The problem with paper leaf bags is that when they are empty, they collapse as you start to put leaves in them. You can buy fancy cardboard and plastic bag stiffeners, but why bother? Just roll the tops of the bags inward. This holds the top wide open while you dump in leaves and other debris from around the yard.

# Long-Reach Rake

To clean up leaves and debris from under a low deck, attach a section of PVC pipe to an old yard rake with a couple of nuts and bolts. Now it's an easy job to clean under the deck without crawling around or bumping your head!

## TWIG PICKUP ON THE GO

Before mowing, you should go around and pick up fallen twigs and other debris. Inevitably, you will miss some and have to stop and pick them up. To solve this common problem, attach a wastebasket to your mower. Now when wrappers, cans and sticks suddenly appear, just stuff them into your basket.

## SMARTER LEAF COLLECTION

Faced with an abundance of leaves to gather and haul to your local compost site? Rather than buying and filling a ton of plastic leaf bags, save time and effort by raking leaves into a Bagster bag (available at home centers). You can pull the full bag into your trailer, transport the leaves and store the useful bag for the next season.

## DEFUZZ YOUR WINDOW SCREENS

Living in close proximity to cottonwood trees can make getting the "fuzz" off your windows a dreadful yearly chore. Removing it with a shop vacuum or a power washer is slow-going and very hard work.

Here's a faster, easier way: Use a lint roller. Just do a few swipes across the screen surface and the fuzz comes right off. This trick works on spider webs and other debris, too. To clean high screens without having to use a ladder, duct-tape the lint roller to a pole. Works great!

# Fast Window Screen Cleaning

When it's time to switch out the window screens and storms each year, take the opportunity to give the screens a great cleaning using a power washer. It makes short work of even the grungiest screens. Just don't stand too close—too much pressure could damage your screens.

# No More Wet Garage Floor

To prevent your snowblower from dripping on the garage floor in winter, keep it on a plastic washing machine pan (which you can find at a home center). To keep the edge of the pan from breaking when you roll a snow blower onto it, beef it up with two pieces of wood.

Wood fastened to edge

## SAFE BLADE DISPOSAL

When removing caulking, you might wind up burning through a lot of
utility knife blades. To safely dispose of the blades, put them in a soda
can and push the pop top back over the opening to contain them.

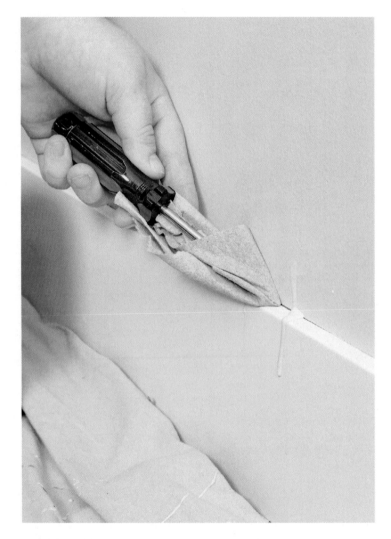

## PRECISION PAINT CLEANUP

If you spill a bit of paint on your trim, fold a piece of cloth around the tip of a screwdriver. Dampen the cloth with the correct solvent, and then wipe the drip away.

# Foil-Tape Paint Saver

After paint cans have been opened and shut over a couple of years, the lids and rims get bent and gooped up, which makes it hard to get an airtight seal. To solve the problem, wrap foil duct tape around the upper part of the can. It works great!

# Super-Fast Floor Squeegee

Here's a classic handy hint for rounding up pesky water on your garage or basement floor. Assemble this simple squeegee by slipping a piece of foam pipe insulation over the tines of a rake. Then just push the water to the drain or out the door.

## MAGNETS FOR CLEAN DRILLING

When you're drilling holes in ferrous metals, stick a rare-earth magnet or two next to the hole you're drilling. The magnets catch the shavings, keeping the waste off the bit, the floor, your clothes and your project. When you're done, use a rag to wipe the shavings off the magnet and into the trash.

# QUICK ROLLER TRAY LINER

Put a layer of aluminum foil in your paint tray before you pour in the paint. This makes cleanup and color changes fast and easy.

# Nature's Drop Cloth

When painting long pieces of trim or siding, do it on the lawn. No drop cloth needed! Any paint drips will disappear the next time you mow the grass.

# No Sawdust in the House!

If your home has a "no sawdust outside the workshop" policy, you'll need a way to keep the sawdust off your clothes. Here's a quick fix. Pick up a pair of nylon athletic pants and a nylon rain jacket at a thrift store, then just slip them over your street clothes when you're kicking up dust in the shop. Nothing sticks to them, and your clothes might last longer, too!

## SAND YOUR HANDS

Some types of wood filler can be hard to get off your hands after they dry, especially if you use your fingers to push it into tiny, tight cracks and holes. When that happens, reach for some fine-grit sandpaper to sand it off your fingers. The paper's also great for removing dried-on polyurethane glue and canned foam from your hands.

## PLASTIC BAG PAINT CONTAINERS

When completing a multicolor paint project, you could find yourself constantly cleaning brushes and containers whenever you switch colors. Do it the smart way by putting the paint in zip-close bags. When it is time to change colors, all you'll have to do is change the bag in the paint bucket. It's a great way to save time and cleanup when you're using a lot of colors for a small paint job.

## POWER FILTER CLEANER

Get the dust out of shop vacuum filters by holding a random-orbit sander (just the pad, without sandpaper) against the filter. This is best done outdoors or with the filter inside a trash bag to keep the dust under control.

# Wine Cork Caulk Saver

Synthetic wine corks are great for sealing partially used tubes of caulk. Drill a 5/16-in. hole into the cork about 1-in. deep. The cork fits perfectly and makes an airtight seal.

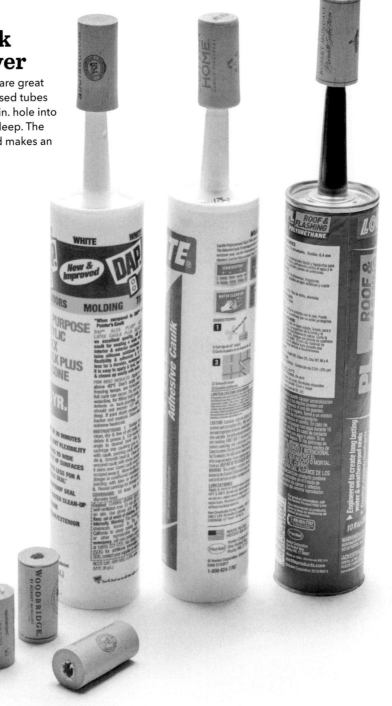

Carabiner  NOT CLIMBING  Zip tie

# Vacuum Cord Control

Do you hold your vacuum cleaner cord in your free hand so your feet don't get tangled in it while you vacuum? Try this: Clip a carabiner onto the handle and then loop the cord through the carabiner. If the carabiner doesn't fit around your handle, you can zip-tie it into place.

# VACUUM COMB

A paintbrush comb is perfect for removing thread that gets wrapped around a vacuum's beater bar and for cleaning things like lint and hair from the bristles.

## INSTANT INK REMOVER

Alcohol-based hand sanitizers do a good job of removing permanent marker ink. They reactivate the ink, allowing you to easily wipe off the stain. Cover the entire ink stain with hand sanitizer. Let it sit for about a minute and then wipe off the ink with a soft rag.

## EASY STICKER REMOVAL

Years-old stickers don't have to be a headache to remove if you follow this simple tip. Soften the adhesive with a blow dryer, and then just scrape them off with a plastic putty knife. No more stickers on the wall!

# Cleaning Wood Stove Glass

Here's the perfect way to clean the glass on the door of a wood stove: Just use the ashes from the stove. Dip a damp paper towel in the cold ashes and rub them on the glass in a circular motion (much like waxing a car). Before you know it, the glass is clean. If the glass has any stubborn stains, wet the glass and carefully scrape them off with a razor scraper.

## Steam-Clean Your Microwave

Many believe steam is the best way to clean a microwave, but don't use plain old water. Here's an extra-special mix: Combine 2 cups of water, 2 tablespoons of vinegar and some lemon rinds in a microwave safe bowl. Microwave the mixture on high for about five minutes, and then, with the door still closed, let it sit for three minutes more. Remove the bowl and wipe down the interior with a sponge.

## NO-ODOR DISPOSER

Tired of a foul-smelling garbage disposer? When your liquid laundry jugs are empty, rinse them and pour the leftover suds down your garbage disposer. No more stinky sink!

## EASY-CLEAN GARBAGE CAN

Food juices leaking from your garbage bags into the bottom of your garbage bin make a nasty and smelly mess. Place newspapers—or even sawdust in the bottom of the bin, under the bag, to soak up liquids and make cleanup easier.

## ELECTRIC GROUT CLEANING

Always save your worn-out electric toothbrush heads. They are perfect for cleaning the grout between shower tiles. Jus apply a little bit of detergent to the head of the brush; it works especially well on corners.

## FRESH, CLEAN DISHWASHER

Once a month or so, add a cup of vinegar to your empty dishwasher and let it run a full cycle. Your kitchen may smell a bit like a pickle jar for a few hours, but hard-water lime buildup will be rinsed away, freeing up the spray arm and other dishwasher parts.

# Catch Detergent Drips

To prevent laundry detergent from dripping on your floor, add a wire handle to the cup. Poke two holes in the cup, thread wire through the holes and hang the cup from the detergent spout to catch any bothersome drips.

Bucket spins
360 degrees
within frame

# ALL-ABOARD SHOP VACUUM

**LONGING FOR A SHOP VACUUM** that won't tip over, stores the hose between jobs and carries extra nozzles and cleaning products right on board? Here it is: a plywood carryall made from scrap 1/2-in. and 3/4-in. plywood. The bucket spins 360 degrees in the frame like the turret on an army tank. Use these dimensions as a guide and adjust them to fit your shop vacuum.

1. First, screw together a 10-in.-high plywood frame 1/4 in. larger than the bucket's diameter. Cut ovals in the 1/2-in. sides for handles. Screw the frame to a 1/2-in. plywood floor, leaving extra space around three sides for storage.

2. Next, drill holes in short pieces of 3/4-in. plywood to hold pieces of PVC pipe to store the hose and nozzles. Use 1-1/2-in. PVC for a 2-in.-diameter hose. A 1-7/8-in. hole saw creates tightly fitting holes for the pipe.

3. Now screw swiveling wheels under the floor of the cart, and get to work cleaning.

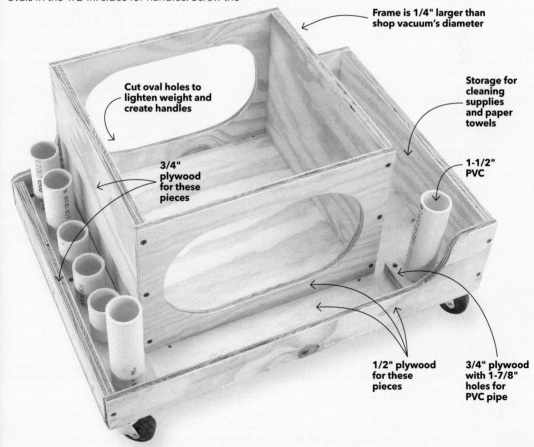

Frame is 1/4" larger than shop vacuum's diameter

Cut oval holes to lighten weight and create handles

Storage for cleaning supplies and paper towels

3/4" plywood for these pieces

1-1/2" PVC

1/2" plywood for these pieces

3/4" plywood with 1-7/8" holes for PVC pipe

# SIMPLY CLEAN

## Tools, tricks and recipes for a spotless home

**SCHAR WARD CLEANS** the good old-fashioned way with homemade cleaning solutions, rags made from sheets and a little elbow grease. With decades of experience, she's tackled dirt, grime and stains that aren't for the faint of heart, and she doesn't think you need fancy new products to clean. With a little knowledge, you can get the job done with many of the household cleaners you probably have lying around. Here are some of her favorite techniques to make your house shine.

**MEET THE EXPERT**
**Schar Ward has been professionally cleaning homes since 1973. She's the author of *Teaching Children t***
***Clean* and loves to pass on her knowledge to the next generation.**

## Run the Dishwasher with Vinegar

Dishwashers need to be cleaned if you have hard water. Place a half cup of vinegar on the top rack and run it normally. Do this every few weeks.

## Ditch the Mop

Schar doesn't use a wet mop. She says mops do more harm than good, spreading dirt everywhere. Instead, she says to clean floors on your hands and knees. First vacuum, then fill a bucket three-quarters full of warm water and 1 Tbsp. Castile soap. Wash with a terry cloth rag in a 4-sq.-ft. section, dry and repeat, working your way out of the room.

## Prevent Mineral Buildup with a Squeegee

Hard water buildup means hard work later. Schar gives a squeegee to all her customers and tells them to use it after every shower. It makes cleaning showers much easier.

# Don't Get Overwhelmed

Faced with a whole house to clean, you're more likely to procrastinate, get sidetracked during the job or just give up. Schar's strategy makes cleaning manageable and efficient.

**START WITH THE DIRTIEST ROOM FIRST**
Tackle the big project first and everything else will seem easy in comparison.

**WORK TOP TO BOTTOM, LEFT TO RIGHT**
You might not know where to start with a dirty room, but Schar says you should work top to bottom, left to right.

**SET A TIME LIMIT**
Instead of telling the family it's a cleaning day, set a time limit. Cleaning isn't so bad when you do it for two hours rather than all day.

**MAKE YOUR OWN RAGS**
Schar makes her own rags from sheets she buys at the thrift store. Cut them to size and, if you like, hem them so they don't fray.

**WASH YOUR RAGS TWICE**
A clean house needs clean rags. Dirty rags harbor all kinds of bacteria, so wash your rags twice—once with bleach and once without.

**FORGET DISPOSABLE CLOTHS**
Use a flannel cloth with a little Old English. It's just as effective and you'll save money.

**ANYTHING YOU WASH, YOU DRY**
Don't wash surfaces with a cleaner and let them dry on their own; it leaves a sticky residue. Dry everything after washing.

**LIFT OBJECTS; DON'T SLIDE**
When dusting, it's easy to move your objects around without thinking about how you're moving them, but Schar emphasizes how important it is to lift them rather than sliding. Sliding scratches the finish.

# Schar's Secret Weapons

Shown below are Schar's favorite commercial cleaning products for removing stubborn mineral deposits, cleaning and protecting wood surfaces and more. It was a surprise to learn that for most cleaning tasks, she prefers to mix her own solutions. Check those out at right.

### 1. PHOSPHORIC ACID CLEANER

For mineral deposits on natural stone, porcelain, concrete and masonry, Schar says phosphoric acid cleaner is a must-have. After applying, let it sit for 10 minutes, rinse and you're done. You could use vinegar, but it takes longer.

### 2. MURPHY OIL SOAP

Schar loves using this cleaner on wood floors, but she makes it clear that you need to dry the floor afterward.

### 3. FOLEX

Schar has seen plenty of tough carpet stains. She says Folex carpet spot remover has never failed to take out a stain. You can find it online or at home centers.

### 4. OLD ENGLISH

To clean and protect your wood surfaces, Schar recommends Old English. Its nongreasy formula helps to prevent water marks and stains.

### 5. USE ERASER SPONGES ON PAINT WITH CAUTION

Familiar eraser sponges like the Magic Eraser have their uses, but be careful on painted surfaces; they can alter the sheen of the paint. Alternatively, use a mix of Murphy Oil Soap and baking soda to clean walls.

# Make Your Own Cleaning Solutions

Instead of loading up on expensive cleaners, make your own solutions with common household products like vinegar and baking soda. Here are a few of Schar's recipes:

## 1. ALL-PURPOSE SPRAY

Fill a spray bottle with a mix of half vinegar and half water. Add 10 drops of scented oil.

## 2. WINDOW CLEANER

Use club soda in a spray bottle.

## 3. SCRUBBING SOLUTION

- 1-3/4 cups baking soda
- 1/2 cup water
- 1/2 cup Castile soap
- A few drops of essential oil

Mix in a bowl and stir until it has the consistency of frosting. Store solution in a pump bottle. Shake well before use. It's effective on pots and pans, sinks, and more.

## 4. HARD-WATER BUILDUP CLEANER

- 1 tsp. borax
- 1 Tbsp. Castile soap
- 2 Tbsp. white vinegar
- 2 cups water
- 5 drops of essential oil

Mix and store the cleaner in a spray bottle.

## 5. CARPET FRESHENER

Fill a shaker container three-quarters full of baking soda. Add 10 drops of essential oil. Mix with a fork and sprinkle on carpet. Clean with a vacuum.

## 6. ESSENTIAL OILS

Add an essential oil to your solutions for a fresh scent.

# CHAPTER 2

ORGANIZATION

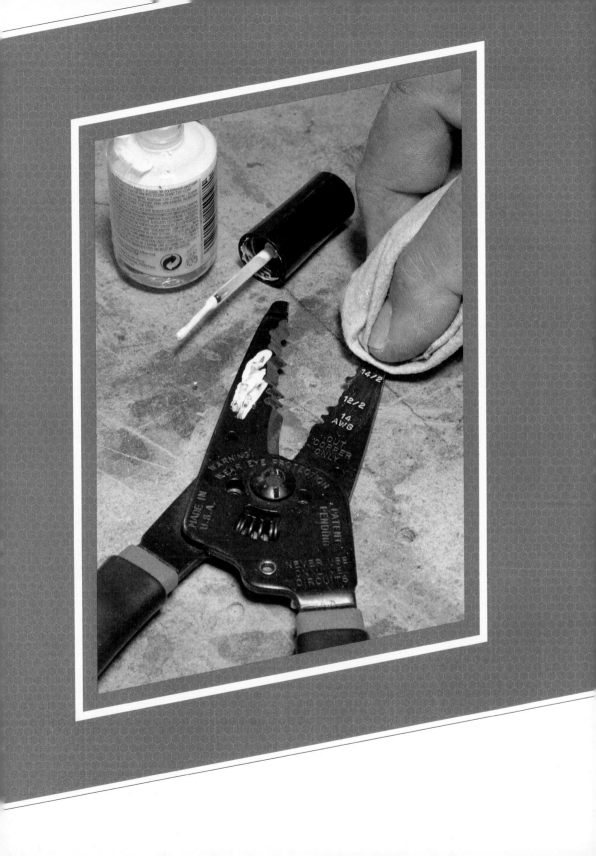

## CAKE-PAN HARDWARE SORTER

This timesaving device, made from an old baking pan, helps you sort through your fastener jar with ease. Using a bimetal hole saw fixed in a drill press, drill a hole slightly smaller than your jar opening. Carefully file and then sand the sharp cut edge. Now you can pour the contents of the jar into the pan, find what you need and then rake the contents through the hole back into the jar.

# Drill Bit Savers

If you carry Forstner drill bits in your toolbox, you'll want to protect those cutting edges. Customize plastic pill bottles by drilling holes in the lids to hold the shank. This also works great for router bits!

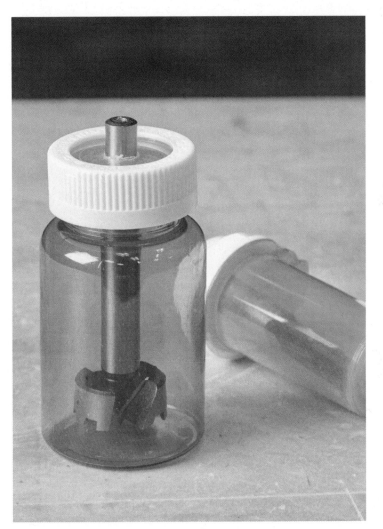

# Simple Paintbrush Drying Rack

This rack is a great place to let paintbrushes drip dry after washing. Just notch a couple of pieces of 1-by material and attach them to a cross support. Pound in some nails and set the rack on top of your sink edge.

# RECIPROCATING SAW BLADE BINDER

Keeping all your reciprocating saw blades inside your saw's case can get messy, and can be hard to find the right one. Snag a binder ring at an office supply store to keep the blades together, and just like that, the problem's solved.

## EASY DRILL HANGER

Pegboard is a great material to hang tools in your shop. Rather than buying special large hooks to hang your drill, just tighten a screw eye in the chuck. This way, you can hang it on a standard small hook or a nail in the wall.

# Neat Sheet Organizer

An expanding file from an office supply store is all you need to keep sandpaper organized by grit. It also has plenty of room to stash your instruction manuals, warranties and other paperwork.

# Stir-Stick Paint Organizer

When you buy custom-mixed paint, the paint clerk slaps the mix label on top of the can. Next time you're getting paint for a project, ask for an extra label to wrap around a stir stick. When you're done with the project, let the stir stick dry and drill a hole near the top of it. Then label both the stick and the can with the name of the room where you used the paint. Hang the stir sticks near cans of leftover paint. With both the color formula and a dried paint sample in view, you don't have to pull down every can to find the right one for touch-ups.

# GARDEN RAKE RECYCLING

Don't put your old rake out to pasture. Put it to use in your workshop instead. Just cut off the handle and hang it on the wall or on your pegboard. It's a handy place to store all of your wrenches and other useful tools.

# PAPER TOWEL CLAMP

It's always nice to have a roll of shop towels at hand when at your workbench. To stop towels from rolling off the bench, attach a quick-grip–style clamp to the edge of the bench, and then slip the paper towel roll over the clamp's rod.

## Better Bit Holder

Toothbrush holders make great, inexpensive holders for drill and driver bits. You can find them at discount stores and drugstores in the sample/travel section. Label the holders with a permanent marker and keep them in your drill tote or tool pouch.

# Instant Labels for Parts Drawers

Plastic drawers let you see the nails or screws inside, but you can't always tell their size. Here's a simple solution: Cut the labels off fastener boxes and tape them inside the front of each drawer. You'll know exactly where everything is located at a glance.

# AIR ACCESSORY ORGANIZATION

Here's an easy way to keep your air compressor accessories organized and easily accessible. Drill 7/16-in. holes on the underside of your workbench top and thread in a few 1/4-in. NPT male couplings with quick-connect couplers. A wrench and some upward pressure are all it takes to screw the couplings into the wood. Now you can just snap those accessories onto the couplers when you're not using them.

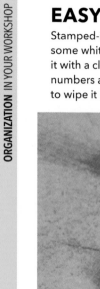

# EASY-TO-READ TOOL MARKINGS

Stamped-in tool markings can be tough to read. To solve this, buy some white fingernail polish, brush it on the tool and quickly wipe it with a clean cloth. The white polish stays in the grooves, and the numbers are easy to read at a glance. You can use lacquer thinner to wipe it if the polish dries too quickly.

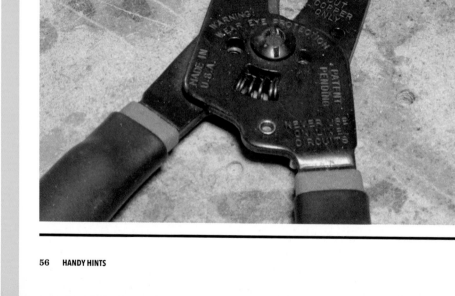

# Pet Collar Cord Hanger

You might not think to look at the pet store for cord hangers, but collars for dogs and cats make great straps to keep the electrical cords and air hoses organized in your shop. Buy several; the leash ring is perfect for hanging the cords on the hooks, and the quick-release fastener makes for fast cord strapping and unstrapping.

# Organizer for Spray Paint

Don't throw away old shoe caddies—turn them into spray paint organizers instead. Just screw the shoe caddy to a wall in the garage, and store all your spray-paint cans in it. This lets you find the color you want, and all those cans aren't taking up your valuable shelf space.

# COLOR-CODED WRENCHES

Colored vinyl tape is a great way to identify your wrenches by type.
Wrap a strip of blue tape around the handle of metric wrenches and
red tape around the SAEs. Don't cover the handle; just put a strip of
tape once around at one end so you don't cover up the size marking.

# MISCELLANEOUS HARDWARE HOLDER

To keep track of small parts, carry quart-size zippered plastic bags in your toolbox. They're a perfect place to store bits and pieces of things you're taking apart. Just write what's inside on the front of the bag, and you'll have everything in one spot when you get around to putting the item back together again.

# Coffee Bag Ties

Small bags of fancy coffee have heavy-duty ties to keep them airtight. Those ties are handy for securing small coils of electrical cable and rope. They're usually fastened to the bag with a dab of glue, making them pretty easy to pull off.

## Second Life for Old Baking Sheets

If you have beat-up old cookie sheets that aren't usable for baking anymore, recycle them by using them in your shop. They're great for preventing a mess when you're doing small-engine repairs or other greasy jobs. They work well for small painting jobs too.

## Six-Pack Shop Organizer

Six-pack cartons are useful for storing and transporting items such as spray paint, lubricants and caulk.

# EASY-FIND SCREWDRIVERS

Finding the right screwdriver is never easy if all the handles look alike. So, to help you identify all your screwdrivers at a glance, use a permanent marker to label the handles with their size and type. Use an "X" for a Phillips head and a dash for a flat-head.

# GUTTER SHELVES

Vinyl rain gutters are fairly inexpensive and great for storing small items. They come in 10-ft.-long sections, so you can cut them up with a power miter saw or hacksaw and make several shelves out of them. Just snap an end cap on each end, drill a couple of holes and attach them to cabinets with wood screws and finish washers. For heavier stuff, attach them with fascia gutter brackets, which you'll find at the home center right next to the gutters.

# Instant Kitchen Cabinet Organizer

A metal file organizer is perfect for storing baking sheets, cutting boards and pan lids. You can pick one up for a buck at the dollar store. To keep the organizer from sliding around, use rubber shelf liner or attach hook-and-loop tape to the cabinet base and the bottom of the organizer.

# Bin Index

It's easy to fall in love with large plastic bins. But remembering what's inside each one is tough, and reading a small label is nearly impossible when your bins are stored high on garage shelves. Solve both problems by labeling bins with large numbers. Each number should correspond to a page in a binder that lists the contents of each bin. It's simple to change the list, and it's a heck of a lot easier to find what you need by checking the binder than by rummaging through each bin.

# HANDY HAT HANGER

An abundance of caps makes it hard to keep them organized in a small space. Take some clothesline, slip a bunch of clothespins over the line through the springs and tie the line to a couple of eye hooks along a wall of your garage. It's a great way to store them and to let them air out.

# ORNAMENTS BY THE CUP

It's hard to store fragile ornaments without breaking them. Try this solution: Use a plastic storage container and store each ornament in a separate plastic cup. By using cardboard to separate the layers, you can stack a lot of ornaments in one sturdy box without any tangling or breaking. You can reuse the same cups and cardboard year after year.

# PVC PLASTIC BAG DISPENSER

Extra PVC pipe can easily turn into a home for grocery bags to reuse. Stuff the bags into the top and pull them out the bottom when you need one. Attach the pipe to the door inside a pantry or closet, or to a wall of your workshop or garage.

# Under-Sink Clutter Control

The space under a kitchen sink is often a black hole where cleaning supplies go to be forgotten. You want to keep this stuff close at hand, but drawers and shelving aren't usually an option because the sink, garbage disposal and plumbing are in the way. But the solution is simple: Insert a curtain tension rod across the cabinet box, and then hang spray bottles, rags and other cleaning supplies on the rod.

# Colorful Key Station

When the kids outgrow their Lego bricks, repurpose a few of them to make this handy key station. Predrill holes in the small bricks to thread in eye screws, and then slip the key rings onto the eye screws. Fasten the base to the wall with some screws, and you're done!

## SHOE SOLUTION

If you have a coat rack in your entryway, you might be surprised to know it works the same for shoes as it does for jackets. To cut down on clutter in front of your door, install another coat rack just for the purpose of hanging up shoes.

1-1/2" SHEET ROCK SCREWS
2x4s
WOOD GLUE
GOLDEN OAK STAIN
80 GRIT SANDPAPER

## SIMPLE NOTE CLIP

Mousetraps make good note clips. You can tack one on the wall over your workbench and fasten them near every stationary tool around your shop—they're really effective and cheap.

# Free Up Closet Space

To make space in your closet, hang hangers in a vertical, cascading fashion. Slide a pop-can tab over the hook of one hanger to create a hook for the next hanger.

## Emergency Labels

It's a good idea to label all the important switches and valves around the house with shipping labels. These include the main water shut-offs and the well electric switch. Then, take photos of all the shut-offs with the tags attached and put them in a "House Reference" binder. If there's a leak when you're not home, everyone will know what to do to prevent a disaster.

# CONVENIENT CORD LABELS

You crawl underneath your desk to unplug something, only to find six different cords—and you have no clue which is the one you're after. Here's a simple idea: Label each cord with a piece of tape. It makes finding the one you need a snap.

## ELECTRICAL CIRCUIT ID

Doing electrical work at home gets a lot safer when you use this labeling technique. Take some time to identify which electrical circuit breaker controls the current to each and every outlet and switch, then remove each cover plate. On the back of the cover plates, write the number of the corresponding circuit breaker. Now, when you change a fixture or do other electrical work, you can unscrew the plate and see which breaker you need to shut off before you even start.

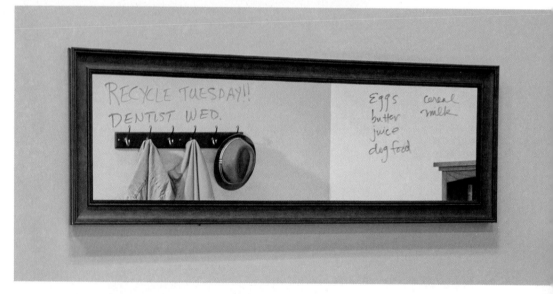

## MIRROR AND MESSAGE BOARD

Staying in touch can be tough, especially if your family is constantly on the go (whiteboards are a solution, but they aren't the best-looking). Buy a full-length mirror, turn it on its side and mount it on the wall. Now you can write on it with dry-erase markers and give yourselves one last look before heading out for the day.

# Temporary Valet Rod

If you need temporary clothes-hanging space around the house, keep an extra shower-tension bar handy. Put it between the jambs in the laundry room door on heavy laundry days. It's also useful in a closet to pack for trips. Or stick it in the closet opening in the guest room/den so overnight guests can hang up their clothes. It's a quick and easy way to gain an extra closet!

# ONE-HOUR DRAWER ORGANIZER

## Dowels and pegboard can keep your pots and pans in order

**OUR KITCHEN DRAWERS** used to have all kinds of pans crammed in however they'd fit. And of course, always seemed as if the one we needed was at the bottom of the pile.

This simple drawer organizer makes everything neat and easily accessible. To make one, cut a piece of 1/8-in. pegboard to fit into the bottom of the drawer. Next, cut 1/2-in.-diameter dowels 6 to 8 in. long. Drill pilot holes in the dowel ends, and then attach them in rows from underneath using 1-in. screws. I used three dowels per row to accommodate any size pan.

Dowel

Pegboard

# 10 USES FOR WIRE COAT HANGERS

## 1. STOP CAULK-TUBE OOZE

To prevent caulk from oozing from the tube once your job is done, trim a 3-in. piece of coat hanger wire; shape one end into a hook and insert the straight end into the tube. Now you can easily pull out the stopper as needed.

## 2. SECURE A SOLDERING IRON

Keeping a hot soldering iron from rolling away and burning something on your workbench is a real problem. To solve this, twist a wire coat hanger into a holder for the iron. To build the holder, simply bend an ordinary coat hanger in half to form a large V. Then bend each half in half so that the entire piece is shaped like a W.

## 3. EXTEND YOUR REACH

Can't reach that pesky utensil that has fallen behind the refrigerator or stove, no matter how hard you try? Here's a fix: Straighten a wire coat hanger (except for the hook at the end), and use it to fish for the object.

## 4. MAKE A GIANT BUBBLE WAND

Kids will love to make giant bubbles with a homemade bubble wand built from a wire coat hanger. Shape the hanger into a hoop with a handle and dip it into a bucket filled with one part liquid dishwashing detergent in two parts water. Add a few drops of food coloring to make the bubbles more visible.

## 5. CREATE ARTS AND CRAFTS

Make mobiles for kids' rooms using wire coat hangers; paint them in bright colors. Or use hangers to make wings and other accessories for costumes.

## 6. UNCLOG TOILETS AND VACUUM CLEANERS

If your toilet is clogged by a foreign object, fish out the culprit with a straightened wire coat hanger. Use a straightened hanger to unclog a jammed vacuum cleaner hose.

## 7. MAKE PLANT MARKERS

Need some waterproof markers for your plants? Cut up little signs from a milk jug or similar rigid but easy-to-cut plastic. Write the name of the plant with an indelible marker. Cut short stakes from wire hangers. Make two small slits in each marker and pass the wire stakes through the slits. Neither rain nor sprinkler will obscure your signs.

## 8. HANG A PLANT

Wrap a straightened wire coat hanger around a 6- to 8-in. flowerpot, just below the lip; twist it back on itself to secure it, then hang the flowerpot.

## 9. MAKE A MINI-GREENHOUSE

To convert an ordinary window box into a mini-greenhouse, bend three or four lengths of coat hanger wire into U's and place the ends into the soil. Punch small holes in a dry-cleaning bag and wrap it around the box before putting it back in the window.

## 10. MAKE A PAINT CAN HOLDER

When you are up on a ladder painting your house, one hand is holding on while the other is painting. How do you hold the paint can? Grab a pair of wire snips and cut the hook plus 1 in. of wire from a wire hanger. Use a pair of pliers to twist the 1-in. section firmly around the handle of your paint can. Now you have a handy hanger.

NOTE These tips work best with wire coat hangers.

# CHAPTER 3

MAINTENANCE

# A BETTER WAY TO REPLANT

When bringing home some new flowers or shrubs for your garden, avoid yanking them out of their plastic pots by the stems—that can hurt the plants. Instead, use a sharp knife to cut down two or more sides of each pot to free the plant, being careful not to tear the roots when separating the soil from the container.

# Wine-Bottle Watering

To keep a plant watered while you're away for a few days, rinse an empty wine bottle and fill it with water. Before you leave, water the plant as usual. Then push the upside-down bottle into the soil, holding your thumb over the bottle's opening until it's buried. Water slowly drains from the bottle as the soil dries.

# Recycle Water

If you have a dehumidifier, you also have a free supply of water that's perfect for houseplants. By removing moisture from the air, dehumidifiers create "condensate" that's free from chemicals and minerals found in tap water. Just don't drink it —it could contain microbes and trace amounts of metals that are harmful to humans.

## SIMPLE PESTICIDE

Whip up a super-simple solution of bleach-free dish soap and water, then spray the mixture on your plants to kill unwanted insects like aphids, mites, thrips and whiteflies.

# ROLL-ON WEED KILLER

Trying to get rid of pesky weeds growing up through the cracks in a patio or walkway? The overspray from spray-on weed killer can damage healthy grass and plants growing nearby. A better solution is to pour some of your premixed weed killer into a paint tray and use a cheap paint roller to roll it directly on the weeds. This prevents overspray and makes it easy to go around patio corners. Make sure to dispose of the roller properly when you're done.

Transmission funnel

Dowel

# Fast Route to the Roots

To get liquid fertilizer down to the plant roots where it will do the most good, you can create your own watering device. Drill holes into the sides of a long plastic transmission funnel (available at any auto parts store). Then sharpen a dowel to a fine point and stick it through the hole of the funnel to make it easier to drive in. When it's time to fertilize, push the funnel into the soil near the plant and pour in water and fertilizer. The mixture runs out through the holes and down to the roots.

# Garden Rock Sifter

Don't give up on your messy river rock mulch, no matter how much dirt and debris is mixed in; make a garden sifter to separate rocks from the debris. Build a 2x4 frame and fasten hardware cloth to the bottom with fence staples. Then elevate the sifter on old bricks and use a power washer to clean each shovelful of rocks. You could also use a hose to spray, or shake the rocks on the sifter (but that's a lot more work!).

# HOLEY WEED BUCKET

Don't throw away the plastic pots from potted plants. With a rope handle attached, they make great weed buckets to carry with you as you tend flower beds or your vegetable garden.

# MINI GREENHOUSES

If you grow plants from seed, you can make great use of the clear plastic containers from tomatoes and other produce. Make them into miniature greenhouses. They have holes for air and drainage, so all you need to do is add soil and plant seeds. When the seedlings grow tall, leave the lid open until it's time to transplant them into the garden. You can reuse the containers year after year.

# SPOT-WATERING TIP FOR GRASS SEED

When you need to water newly seeded patches throughout your lawn, it can be tough to remember where you've spread the seed. Give yourself a visual reminder by lightly topping the new grass seed with small-animal bedding. It will keep the newly seeded areas moist, the grass will grow right through the bedding and you'll immediately see where you need to water.

# Flowerpot Filler

Water settling at the bottom of pots can lead to root rot from poor aeration. To combat this, toss a few old sponges in the bottom of the pot. The sponges retain moisture and create necessary air space. They also help prevent water from running out the bottom.

# Shady Flower Shelf

Here's an idea for sprucing up the crotch of a tree. Make yourself a shady plant shelf! Just measure the gap and cut your shelving to fit. Cut a notch in each side of your board so that it "hugs" the tree and sits securely. Set your shelf gently inside the crotch of your tree, place your shade-loving plants on it and enjoy your beautiful blooms all season long.

## POISON YOUR IVY, NOT YOUR SHRUB

Here's a clever way to get rid of twining briars and nuisance vines without damaging your shrubs. Buy a few floral water tubes (available at floral supply companies and nurseries) or just reuse the tubes that come with individual roses. Fill the floral tube with a little herbicide (like Roundup) and replace the rubber cap to keep out pets and rain. Stick the tube in the ground and then stick the tip of the vine into the tube. The vine will "drink up" the weed killer down to its roots and die within a few days.

## ZIP-TIE VINE TRAINERS

It can be challenging to tie your vines to a trellis without damaging
the vine. Cable ties (also called zip ties; about $5 for 100 at home
centers) are a good way to solve this problem, especially for tomatoes.
They're easier to use than twine, and also waterproof, strong and
adjustable. You can make the tie loose enough to give the vine room
to grow, yet tight enough that it doesn't flop. (Just don't make them
too tight—you might damage the stem.)

# Easier Mulching

If you're putting in a new garden this spring, here's a tip that will help your seedlings. After your new plants are in the ground, cover each one of them with a used nursery pot. Then pour your mulch around each pot. Your delicate seedlings won't get buried, and they'll be mulched perfectly when you remove the pots.

# Under-the-Hood Maintenance Record

A truck's air filter cover makes a perfect blackboard for a maintenance schedule. Use a chalk marker to write down the dates you last changed the oil, air filter, spark plugs, etc. The chalk marker isn't affected by water but is easily cleaned off with an ammonia-based cleaner (such as Windex). This is much simpler than recording everything in the owner's manual. It's right where you need it!

## TEMPORARY PROTECTION FOR EXTENSION CORDS

Extension cords on damp ground can trip ground-fault circuit interrupters, which is frustrating. Instead of pushing the reset button every couple of minutes, cut notches in a plastic container and place the plug connection inside. Drill a couple of 1/4-in. holes in the bottom of the container so any water that gets in can drain out.

## EASIER LAWN MOWER OIL DRAINING

Here's a neat trick to make lawn mower oil changes a lot easier. Older gas mowers had a drain plug to remove used oil. But with many newer mowers, you have to turn the mower on its side to drain the oil, which is awkward. Instead of doing that, clamp plastic tubing to a turkey baster and use it to drain the oil. Stick the end of the tubing into the oil fill hole and suck out the oil. Squirt the used oil into an oil can and repeat as many times as it takes to empty it.

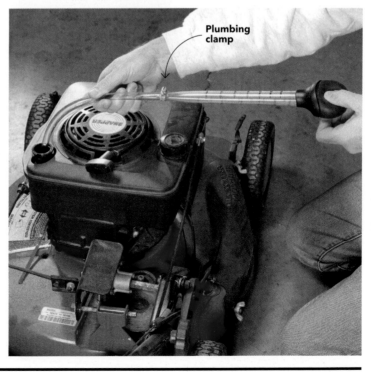

Plumbing clamp

## WATER BREAK ON THE GO

Coming into the house for a drink of water when you're hard at work mowing the lawn is no fun. Attach a bicycle water bottle holder to the mower arm to solve the problem. Fill up the bottle at the start and take water breaks whenever you need.

## DAMS IN A GARAGE

Garages without drains might require a way to contain water from melting snow. Do this by making a dam around the car with minimal-expanding spray foam insulation. Just scrape it off when spring returns.

# Hose Connection Extender

If your hose bib is nestled among a variety of prickly and thorny bushes, this tip will save time (and your arms and legs!). By running plastic pipe inside a PVC fence post and attaching a hose bib and a nipple, you can solve this problem quickly and easily. Run a short piece of garden hose from the existing connection to the nipple, and now the water supply is right where you need it. To keep the post stable, run some threaded rod crosswise through the bottom of the post, dig a shallow hole and sink the post in concrete.

# Sidewalk Salt Shaker

Lugging a heavy bag of de-icer out to the sidewalk is no fun, and it's tough to spread de-icer evenly with a shovel or cup. You usually get a clump in one spot and none in another, so you're wasting both time and de-icer. Here's a great solution: Make a sidewalk salt shaker from a big plastic coffee container with a handle. Poke 1/4-in. holes in the lid and fill it with sand, cat litter, de-icer or a mix of whatever you want and shake away!

## SOLAR DECK-LIGHT MOUNTS

Want to put lights on your deck but hate the idea of running wire?
Here's an easy way to mount solar lights and let the sun do the rest
of the work: Remove the bottom plug from the lights and cut a short
length of wooden dowel that fits inside the light tube. Run a screw
up through the bottom of the railing (drill a pilot hole first) and then
up through the dowel. Then just slip the light over the dowel and it
becomes a permanent fixture. Brilliant!

## WINDPROOF TRASH BIN

Sick of picking up trash strewn about the driveway after a big windstorm? It's easy to take action. At the hardware store, pick up a nylon strap, the kind with a buckle. Fasten it to your garage wall with a deck screw and fender washer, loop it around your trash bin's handle, cut it to length and cinch it up. Just like that, no more trash-collecting job for you!

## INSTANT FIRE STARTER

If you need some tinder to start a fire, try corn chips. The corn oil in them is flammable and provides a steady burn that will have your fire blazing in no time. Corn chips—don't go camping without them!

# Easier Gutter Cleaning

To speed up the task of cleaning out your gutters, use a dryer-vent cleaning brush and flexible extension rods. Depending on how many extension rods you use, you can clean 4, 8 or even 12 ft. of gutter from the same spot. Just hook the rod onto your drill, slide the brush under the first bracket and turn it on. As you feed the rod down the gutter, the brush spins and pushes all the debris right over the side.

# Plug Saver

If you're always running extension cords from the garage out to your yard, avoid the hassle of the cord getting unplugged or damaging the plug's prongs. Tie a loose loop in the cord and hang it on a heavy-duty screw hook installed right next to the outlet. The hook keeps the plug connected in case you pull a little too hard on the cord.

# CRITTER-PROOF PROPANE HOSES

Don't let your propane hose become a chew toy for rodents. To prevent this trip to the hardware store and keep your propane hose off the critter menu, wrap the hose with split flexible plastic conduit. And with this fix, pests will have to look elsewhere for their meals in the winter!

# NO-MESS CHARCOAL BAGS

Bags of charcoal are often large, cumbersome and messy. Get around that by storing charcoal in small bags with about 15 to 20 briquettes per bag, perfect for one grilling session.

# Bike Gear To Go

Hunting down all your biking gear when you want to go for a ride can be a bit of a chore. Solve the problem by picking up a plastic crate at a garage sale (or department store). Screw some 2x4 pieces to the back of the crate (use fender washers with the screws to better grip the plastic). Then screw through the studs into the 2x4s. Next, screw a 25-in.-long 2x4 to the front of the top and add a pair of rubber-coated bike hooks. Keep biking shoes, a helmet, gloves, a tire pump and your water bottles within reach so you spend more time biking and less time looking in closets!

# Fence Post Removal

Plenty of different methods exist for removing 4x4 fence posts sunk in concrete, but this one is among the easiest. Screw a piece of scrap 2x4 to the post a couple of inches from the ground, place a landscape timber alongside as a fulcrum, and use a long metal bar as a lever. Just stand on the bar, and the post and concrete footing will usually pop right out of the ground.

# GUTTER INSPECTION

If you have tall trees all around your house, you likely check the gutters several times a year to make sure they're free of leaves and needles. Instead of hauling out the ladder each time, use a gutter inspection tool that makes this chore a breeze. Make it by taping a sideview mirror (which you can find on an old car at the junkyard) to an extension pole. To check the gutters, extend the mirror and get a perfect view without having to leave the ground.

## PROTECT SPRINKLER HEADS IN THE LAWN AND ROCKS

To keep the rocks (or the lawn mower) from interfering with sprinkler heads, protect them with PVC pipe. Cut the pipe into 6-in. lengths and push it into the ground around those heads so the pipe sticks up an inch higher than the heads. This also helps keep leaves and grass clippings from building up around the heads.

# Unclog Your Showerhead

Depending on what kind of showerhead you have, it might get clogged with calcium deposits from hard well water. Removing the showerhead and soaking it overnight in vinegar until the small holes are cleared is one option, but this is faster. Buy a welding tip cleaner at a home center. The cleaner has abrasive needles in a variety of sizes that quickly knock out the mineral chunks from the tiny holes–no need to remove the showerhead.

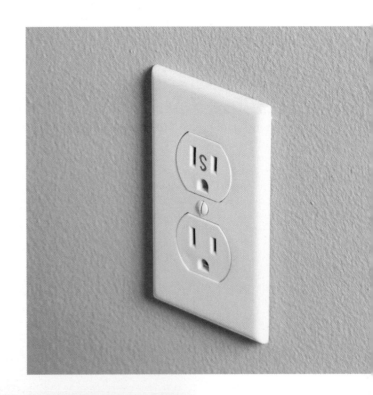

## Easy ID for Switched Outlets

It can be tricky to remember which of your home's outlets are powered by a light switch and which are always live. To eliminate confusion, mark the switched outlet with an "S." No more mix-ups!

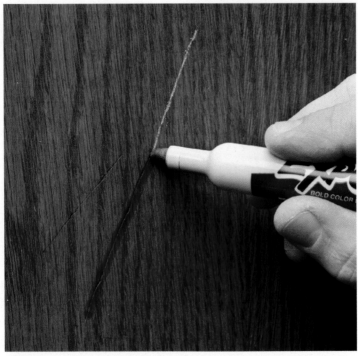

## Wood Scratch Remover

Seeing scratches on your wood door or cabinet? Try brown dry erase markers to make them disappear. Just draw over the scratch and immediately wipe off the excess ink. The worst of the scratch will be covered. Just make sure the shade of brown isn't too dark for your cabinet.

# FAST FIX FOR STICKING DRAWERS

Sticking drawers are as frustrating to homeowners as they are common. To remedy this problem, grab a candle and rub it along the bottom of the drawer, and along the wood runner. Now older drawers will slide like new—and almost as smoothly as fancy new drawers.

# PERFECT PIPE INSULATION

To make fast and accurate cuts in pipe insulation, use a hand miter box and a bread knife. You can get precise 45- and 90-degree cuts for a tight fit and a professional look.

# Golf Ball Sink Stopper

Golf balls are surprisingly good at stopping the water in your sink, and they might be easier to remove than your normal drain plug. To make your own golf ball sink stopper, drill a pilot hole into the center of the ball and attach an eye screw with a string tied on it. Hole in one!

# A Fix for Clicking Ceiling Fans

For those who use ceiling fans, the bead chains tapping against the light fixture can drive you nuts! Thankfully, it's easy to silence them. Just unhook the chains, slip them through lengths of clear 1/4-in. tubing and reattach them. No more chattering chains to contend with.

# INSULATION SUPPORT

Installing ceiling insulation is tricky, especially by yourself. Make it easier by tightening a bar clamp across the rafter bay you're working on to hold up the insulation in the middle. This allows you to work down each side without holding on to the roll.

# FEWER FINGERPRINTS

The next time you clean all of your shiny stainless-steel kitchen appliances, finish the job with a coat of car wax. It not only makes wiping off grime after cooking easier but also inhibits fingerprints. Simply apply a light coat of wax, let it dry and buff with a soft cloth. Apply wax only to the area around the controls, not the cooking surface.

# Low-Cost Chimney Draft Blocker

If you don't use your fireplace that often, here's a simple, inexpensive way to keep warm air from escaping up your chimney. Cut a piece of plywood the same size as your fireplace opening. Paint the plywood with flat black latex paint and let it dry. The plywood will magically disappear when you press it into the dark fireplace opening. You can make simple handles out of small pieces of wood screwed together and painted black.

# Sofa Stops

Felt pads for furniture feet do a great job of protecting wood floors, but they can be pretty hard on walls; they won't stop the sofa from sliding into the wall when you sit down, which can leave ugly scuff marks. To solve that problem, screw two doorstops on the back of the sofa legs at a height that hits the baseboard. That way when the sofa slides, it won't cause damage to the wall.

# QUICK FIX FOR MARKER MISTAKES

Who hasn't accidentally written on a whiteboard with permanent marker? Luckily, it's no sweat to remove. Simply write over the permanent marker ink with a dry-erase marker and then wipe with an eraser or a dry cloth. Your dry-erase board will be as good as new, right away!

## SMARTPHONE SMARTS

Keeping your cellphone clean when painting or working in your garden is hard, especially if you keep it in your back pocket. Don't run out to buy an expensive phone cover—try this easy (and cheap!) solution. Stick it in a zip-top plastic bag. You can still work all the buttons right through the plastic while keeping the phone itself clean and dry.

# Sump Pump Noise Reduction

Some basement sump pumps run pretty often in the spring, and the vibrations are heard all over the house. To dampen the sound, replace a section of the plastic pipe with a radiator hose secured with hose clamps. To ensure you get the right hose size, take a section of pipe to the auto parts store. It works great!

**Radiator hose**

**Hose clamp**

# Last-Ditch Nail Pulling

If you're really trying to pull a nail and the head breaks off, try gripping the nail tightly with a locking pliers, then pull against the pliers.

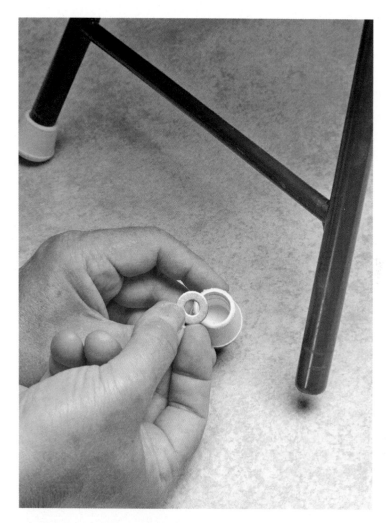

# STOOL LEG PROTECTOR

Stools sometimes have sharp ends that slice through plastic caps. To solve this problem, place a washer the same diameter as the pipe into the plastic cap and then fit it onto the leg. Now the stool will no longer mar the floor.

# FORGET IT ... REGRET IT!

## Ignoring these little jobs can lead to big trouble

### Drain sediment from your water heater ... or expect a shorter life span

Imagine this: You call a plumber because your water heater isn't heating, and furthermore, it's leaking. Right away, the pro will ask if you've been draining some of the water from it every year. If you don't, sediment will collect at the bottom of the tank. A buildup of sediment creates hot spots on gas-powered heaters that can damage the tank and cause premature failure. That buildup can make the lower heating element fail on an electric water heater, so occasionally draining a water heater will lower energy bills and extend the life of the heater. If this has cost you your old water heater, drain your new one at least once a year.

## Check for high water pressure ... or wreck fixtures and appliances

Brand-new water softeners can fail if you're not checking for a key component: water pressure. An old pressure-reducing valve can also be part of the problem, so if yours is a few decades old, you'll need to have it replaced. Pressure-reducing valves are usually found near the main water shutoff valve, but not all homes have them. It depends on your municipality.

High water pressure can harm pipes, connections and appliances, and create water hammer and waste massive amounts of water. Checking for high water pressure is an often overlooked maintenance item, and it's one that's easy enough to perform.

A new pressure-reducing valve costs less than $100, and a simple pressure gauge like the one above that hooks up to a spigot or tub faucet costs about $10. Both are available at home centers—and it's well worth the money to pay for those items now, rather than shelling out cash to replace damaged appliances in the future.

## Check garage door balance ... or wreck your opener

A properly balanced door is less likely to injure someone and keeps the door opener from working too hard, which will shorten the life of the opener.

To check the balance on a door, close the door and then disengage the opener by pulling the opener release handle. Manually pull up the door about halfway and let go. A properly balanced door stays in the halfway position by itself. If it falls, the tension needs to be increased. If the door rises, the door spring has too much tension, which means it's working harder than it needs to.

Check the door a couple of times a year. Adjusting the spring tension is tricky and dangerous, so it's best to research or let a pro handle it. Call a garage door professional to perform the service, or search for "advanced garage door repairs" at familyhandyman.com.

## Lube garage door springs ... or replace them sooner rather than later

Coat the overhead torsion springs mounted above roller tracks with a garage door lubricant. All springs will eventually break because of metal fatigue and/or corrosion, but lubing them at least once a year will make your springs last longer. Spraying can be messy; it's very smart to protect the wall behind the spring you're lubing with a piece of cardboard. Lube the rollers, hinges and track while you're at it. For more garage door maintenance tips, search for "garage door tune-up" at familyhandyman.com.

## Clean dryer vents ... or waste energy and risk a fire

A plugged dryer vent is sure to make your dryer inefficient—and it could cause a house fire! Dryers that are centrally located are prone to plugging because of longer ducts.

Excess lint is only one reason ducts get clogged; nesting pests and stuck exhaust hood flappers can also cause backups. Stronger odors and longer dry times are two signs your vent is plugged.

You'll have to remove the vent from the back of the dryer to clean it. Suck debris from the ducts with a wet/dry vacuum, or ream it out with a cleaning kit that includes a brush on a long flexible rod that attaches to a power drill.

If your ducts need replacing, purchase smooth metal ducts, which will stay cleaner longer than flexible ducts. Avoid using any plastic ducting altogether; it can be a fire hazard.

## Clean refrigerator coils ... or pay for repair bills—or a new fridge

When coils are clogged with dust, pet hair and cobwebs, they can't efficiently release heat. Then your compressor works harder than it was designed to, using more energy and shortening your fridge's life.

Clean the coils with a coil-cleaning brush and vacuum. Coil-cleaning brushes are bendable to fit in tight areas, and they do a thorough job. Look for one online or at appliance stores.

## Clean window weep holes ... or invite rainwater right into your house

Many sliding windows and vinyl replacement windows have weep holes on the exterior bottom of the frame. These holes are designed to drain away rainwater that can collect in the frame's bottom channel. Weep holes can get plugged with bugs and debris; if that happens to yours, water could fill up the channel and spill over into your house.

To see if your weep system is working, simply pour a glass of water into the track or spray the outside of the window with a garden hose. If you don't see a steady stream of clean water exiting the weep hole, poke a wire hanger into the hole, or spray it out with compressed air, and then wet it down again. If the little flapper (designed to keep out driving wind) is stuck shut, it can be removed with a putty knife and replaced.

## Test the sump pump ... or risk a flood

No one wants to get home from a trip to discover their basement floor covered in water. This can have several causes, including a tangled sump pump cable, but one easily neglected item can certainly be the culprit: a rarely tested sump pump.

To avoid future disasters, you might consider buying a pump with a vertical float switch. But most importantly, you'll want to check your pump at least a couple of times a year by dumping water into the basin to make sure everything is working properly. That move will save you time and money (not to mention the headache of taking all of your waterlogged stuff out of the basement after a vacation) down the line.

# CHAPTER 4

DIY HINTS

## PLYWOOD CUTTING GRID

If you want an easier way to cut sheets of plywood into smaller pieces with a circular saw, build this cutting grid from 2x4s. Set your grid on a couple of sawhorses and let the sawdust fly. When you're done, lean it against the wall for next time. You won't need to worry about cutting into a wooden grid, and the screws are located low enough that the blade won't hit them.

# Sure-Grip Push Block

To work with more precision and safety when you're routing, dadoing or jointing workpieces, a grippy push block is the best. To make one, apply rubber shelf liner to a piece of 3/4-in. plywood with contact cement, and then add a handle to maintain downward and forward pressure on the workpiece. For longer workpieces, use two blocks.

# Homemade Detail Sander

It can be hard to sand louvered doors, shutters and other items that have a lot of tight spaces. Oscillating tools with sanding pads work great, but the pads don't always come with the tools and they're expensive to buy. That's why it's a good idea to make your own detail sander using a dull blade and custom-cut sandpaper that's glued on with spray adhesive. When the sandpaper gets dull, just peel it off and stick on a new piece.

# Screw Holder

While doing some remodeling, you may need to spray-paint the switch plate covers and screws so that they match new colors. If you don't have any Styrofoam to hold the screws, use an old advertising sign with corrugated edges (old political signs work, too). Cut a strip, and you'll find that the screws fit perfectly.

# SIMPLE SANDING BLOCK

Not happy with the selection of sanding blocks at the hardware store? Make a few of your own from hardwood scraps left over from a woodworking project. You can cut each one to 3/4 in. x 1-1/2 in. x 4-1/2 in.—which is just the right size to wrap a quarter sheet of sandpaper around. And the "kerf" cut helps hold the sandpaper in place until you're ready to change it.

## CAULK CLAMP

If you're missing your clamps, there's no cause for concern. Your caulk gun makes a great substitute. Put a positioning block on one end to even out the pressure and then squeeze the parts together. No clamps, no problem – it'll work great!

# DIY Simple Angle Template

T-bevels are useful for a variety of angled wood projects, but if you don't have one, it's easy to make them from steel joining plates. Screw through one of the holes in the plate, set your angle, then add another screw to lock the angle. You can then use it as a template to mark all the pieces at the same angle and cut them with a circular saw.

# DIY Fluted Dowels

If you need to glue a dowel and you're out of the fluted version, just make your own. Place a smooth dowel in your vise and drag your hacksaw over it a few times to roughen up the surface. You'll create the grooves that the glue and air need to escape when you drive in the dowel.

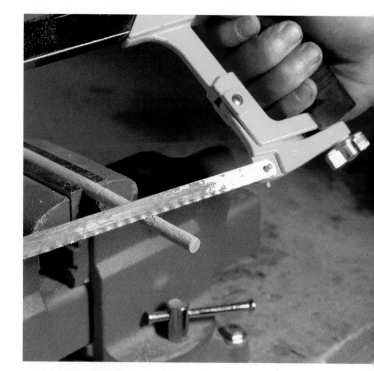

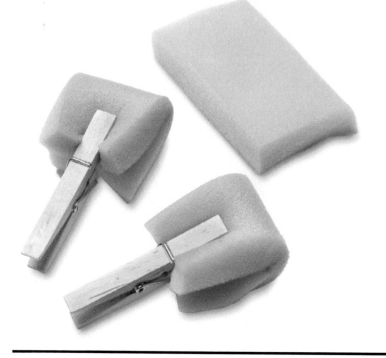

# Cheap and Easy Foam Brushes

Small foam brushes come in handy for projects in your shop. Instead of buying them, make your own out of foam packing material and clothespins. Cut the foam about 1/4-in. thick, and when you're done with them, throw them away.

# FREE FUNNELS

You can use plastic bottles for large-mouth or very fine funnels instead of those purchased from a store. Homemade funnels are disposable/recyclable when no longer needed. Plus, when you find an unusual bottle, you can cut the top off and store it for future use. (Feel free to start a collection in your garage.)

## CUSTOMIZED CARTS

To save time, space and your back, here's a great way to organize and ferry everything you need for different jobs all around the house. Use appliance dollies and bungee cords to create all-in-one carts. Make a compressor cart for nailing jobs, a saw cart with your sawhorses on the back, and a cart of plastic crates loaded with supplies for wiring, painting and other common jobs. These carts make going up and down stairs easier, you don't have to drag along heavy tool cases, and they really cut down the number of trips you make to and from your workshop.

# Built-in Blade Height Gauge

Here's a quick way to set your blade or dado height for non-through cuts on the table saw. Make a scale directly on your table saw's fence using a fine-point permanent marker. You'll have to refresh the marks once in a while—they'll end up getting rubbed off by stock sliding against the fence.

## Ladder Guards

If you're looking to keep your gutters scratch-free, you'll be a big fan of these nifty and simple ladder protectors made out of an old swim noodle (foam pipe insulation would work too). Just cut 2-ft. sections of the foam noodle, slit them with a razor knife and stick them right on the sides of the ladder. They make the perfect cushions! If the foam doesn't stay put, try taping it on.

# NO-MESS PENCIL SHARPENER

Small pencil sharpeners are convenient, but the shavings make a mess unless you sharpen over a trash can. Create a container for shavings by drilling a hole in the lid of a pill bottle, hot-gluing the sharpener to it, and then screwing the lid back on the bottle.

# AN EGG-CELLENT PAINTING TIP

Whenever you need to paint something small like a picture frame and want to raise it off the table a bit to paint the edges, break out these handy egg cartons. Just cut a couple in half and use them to support the frame's edges. You can reuse them several times or just throw them away when you're done.

# Cut a Bolt in Seconds

When you need to shorten a bolt, let your drill do
the work. Put two nuts on the bolt and tighten them
against each other. Then stick the bolt in a drill and
hold a hacksaw against the spinning bolt. The nuts
help to steady the saw blade and remove burrs
when you take them off the bolt.

# Hinge Face-Lift

Going from chrome fixtures to copper in your kitchen often means new matching knobs for the doors and drawers. When it comes to the hinges, it can be difficult to find new ones that fit the old mounting holes, and the choices can be expensive. Painting the hinges metallic copper can work if they aren't handled every day and won't show wear. Just remove the hinges, rub them with steel wool and spray them with metallic paint and a clear coat. The hinges will look great at a fraction of the cost of new.

# GRIP A STRIPPED SCREW HEAD

As long as it's driven completely, a stripped screw head normally isn't a big setback—until you need to remove the screw. So, the next time it happens, try this trick before attempting more destructive measures. Stretch a wide rubber band around the driver tip, then apply as much downward force as possible as you slowly turn the screw. The rubber band often grips the stripped screw head just enough to allow you to back out the screw.

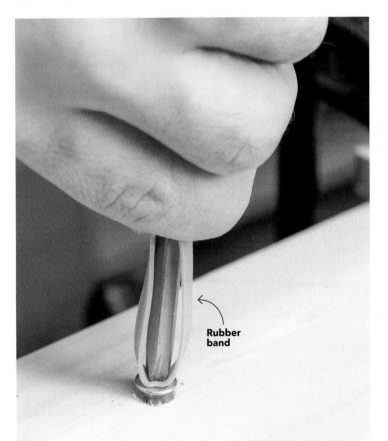

**Rubber band**

## ARTISTIC TOUCH-UPS

Stain markers are a good way to touch up damaged finishes. But if you want a perfect match, stop by an art supply store. They have every color you can imagine. If you get two or three colors, you can match the colors and pattern of wood grain.

## LADDER TOPPER

When you work overhead on a ladder, a heavy tool belt can take a toll on your back and legs. Instead of wearing it, cinch it around the top of the ladder. That'll keep all the tools right where you need them.

# No-Fuss Veneer Trimming

You don't need a special veneer trimmer or a router to trim wood veneer. But don't try to trim the veneer from the finished side. Flip the workpiece over on a flat work surface instead. Then slice the veneer with a sharp utility knife from the back side. If the project is too large to cut on a workbench, hold a backer block against the veneer face to use as a cutting surface.

**Adhesive-backed veneer**

# Perfectly Square, Hands-Free!

Holding parts square while clamping and fastening can be tricky. These plywood triangles make it easy. Using a miter saw or table saw, cut the triangles, taking care that your setup is perfectly square. Drill a hole that's large enough for your clamp heads at each corner. Be sure to cut off the triangle's top corner, so it doesn't get glued to your workpiece.

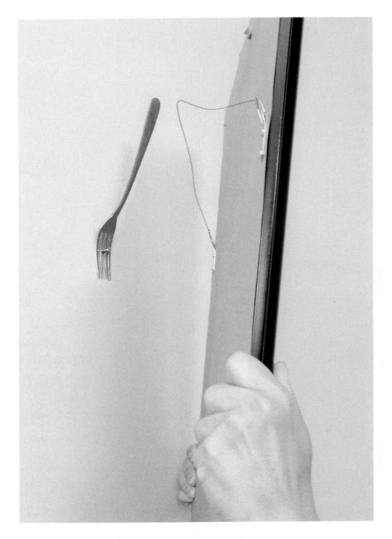

## PICTURE-HANGING HACK

Getting the wire to catch the nail's head isn't always as easy as it sounds. To eliminate frustration, slip a fork onto the nail and slide the wire over the fork until it's hooked on the nail, then pull out the fork.

## SPRING-LOADED HINGE PIN REMOVER

You can mess up the trim around your doors by using a screwdriver and a hammer to pound out stubborn door hinge pins. Instead, try using a spring-loaded nail set to do the job. It takes about three shots and the pin is out. You'll find a spring-loaded nail set for about $35 at rockler.com.

# Sawdust for Oil Spills

Sawdust won't remove the stain from an oil spill, but it can quickly get rid of the puddle. If you have power tools, you've got a ready supply. Sprinkle a generous amount of sawdust over the oil and let the pile sit for about 20 minutes. Using a stiff broom, sweep sawdust over the spill a few times to soak up as much oil as possible. Scoop the oily sawdust into a plastic bag, tie it shut and toss it in the trash. You may need to use a degreaser to remove any oily residue.

**Note:** In most states, it's acceptable to throw oil-soaked sawdust in the trash (as long as the oil is no longer in liquid form). However, you should check your local regulations before doing so.

# Lighted Shop Vacuum

Shop vacuums are often used in dimly lit places, such as under car seats. To make it easy to see what you're doing, zip-tie a small flashlight to the hose. It works like a charm.

# WIRE IN THE HOLE

If you've used masonry screws to attach something to a block wall, you know you have to predrill holes for the screws. But that concrete block is hollow and crumbly, and sometimes a screw won't tighten; it just spins inside the hole. The solution? Back out the screw, put a piece of insulated wire inside the hole and drive the screw alongside it. Then snip off the excess wire. It makes a nice, tight connection!

# A STICKY SOLUTION

To keep a square from sliding on slick material when you're trying to mark with it, stick some vinyl picture-frame bumpers on the back. This holds the square in place while you draw a line.

## STAND-AT-ATTENTION SCREWS

When you need to insert small screws and bolts and keep them positioned until they find their place, use a rare earth magnet attached to the screwdriver shaft. It holds better than the usual magnetized tip. Just keep the magnet stuck inside your tool chest and use it with any size of screwdriver. It's also great for picking up dropped nuts and screws in tight spaces.

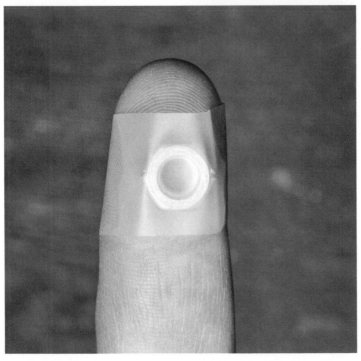

## STICKY FINGER

When you need to screw on a nut in a tight space, hold it on your finger with Scotch tape. That makes it easier to get the screw started (the piece of tape is thin enough for a machine screw to poke through).

# Perfect Pilot Holes

If you're fastening moldings by hand (without a pneumatic finish nailer), you'll need to predrill a hole the diameter of the nail so you don't split the wood. If you don't have a drill bit in the right size, don't worry—predrill using one of the finish nails. Simply clip the head off the nail with wire cutters or lineman's pliers. Then chuck the headless nail into the drill. This will give you the perfectly sized pilot hole every time.

# Wet-Saw Marking Tip

Use a crayon to draw the cutting line on tile before using a wet saw.
Unlike a pen or pencil line, a crayon mark won't wash off and is easier
to see in the muddy water.

## SUPER-COMFY HAMMER GRIP

If you need to replace a worn-out grip on an old hammer or add a grip to a hammer without one, here's a frugal solution. Buy a multipack of tennis racket grips and you'll have a lifetime supply. You can get a five-pack for as little as $8. Racket grips are adhesive-backed and easy to apply. Most grips are also padded, adding to their comfort and reducing the shock of repeated pounding.

## NEW LIFE FOR BROKEN SHOP VACUUMS

Do you have a dead shop vacuum on your hands? Rather than trash the whole thing, toss the lid and motor, and use the canister as a roll-around trash can. Just nudge it with your toe to move it to wherever you need it.

## Renew a Knife Blade

Utility knife blades usually dull near the tip long before the rest of the blade loses its edge. To get more mileage out of a blade, put on a pair of safety glasses and snap off the tip with pliers. Presto! You've got a sharp tip.

## Chain Saw Sharpening Made Easier

When sharpening your chain saw, it's easy to get confused about which teeth have been sharpened and which ones haven't as you pull the chain around the bar. To prevent befuddlement, just mark each tooth with a permanent marker after you've sharpened it.

# Grit Reminder

After remodeling your kitchen, you might wind up with a shoebox full of sanding sponges of various grits and no idea what's what. In the future, before tossing the packaging, write the grit number on the end of the sponge with a permanent marker. You can reuse sponges that have lost their grit by simply wrapping them with sandpaper.

## REPLACEMENT SANDER PAD

If you have a rubber cushion on an old palm sander that's wearing thin around the edge, try using a foam can cover as a replacement pad. Just peel off the old pad, clean the metal base and attach the foam with contact cement. This works for clamp-on as well as stick-on sanding squares. You can find can covers at convenience and discount stores.

# BETTER BLADES IN MINUTES

Pitch buildup on saw blades causes friction, burning and premature blade dulling. You can buy special cleaners that remove the pitch, but this easy fix uses stuff you already have around the house. Heat a pan of water to boiling, drop in the saw blade, and then pour baking soda on the blade. Leave the blade in the boiling water for five minutes or so, then carefully remove it and wipe it dry.

# Easy-on-the-Hands Bucket Handles

Old buckets with broken plastic handles can be tough on your hands. Rather than gritting your teeth through the pain, retrofit the buckets with new handles made from an old garden hose. Cut short lengths of hose, slit each one with a utility knife and slide them over the handles. If you can remove one side of the wire handle, you can just slide the hose on without slitting it.

# Shop Vacuum Organizer

A PVC tee makes the perfect holder for shop vacuum attachments. Take one of your attachments to the home center and find a PVC tee that fits it. Drill a hole in the tee to fit a screwdriver, put a plywood spacer behind it and screw it to the wall.

PVC tee

Hole for mounting screw

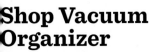

# SUPER-SIMPLE WORKBENCH

**THIS STURDY 30-IN. x 6-FT.-LONG WORKBENCH** is the ultimate in simplicity. It's made from only fifteen 8-ft.-long 2x4s and one sheet of 1/2-in. plywood. Follow the cutting diagrams to cut the parts: **Figure B** to cut the plywood tops, then **Figure C** to cut all the framing. Use the lengths provided in the **Cutting List.** You can either screw the framing together with 3-in. screws or hand- or power-nail it together with 3-in. nails. Screw the plywood down with 1-5/8-in. screws.

To make these project plans even easier to follow, we tinted the parts that get added at each step.

## FIGURE B
## PLYWOOD CUTTING DIAGRAM

Waste

Upper shelf 2' x 12"

Upper shelf 4' x 12"

Lower shelf 18" x 6'

Work surface 30" x 6'

G

A

A

A A

Work surface

E

D

B

Legs

C

Lower shelf

F

B

D

C

A

A

C

## FIGURE A
## MAIN WORKBENCH PARTS

## CUTTING LIST

| KEY | QTY. | SIZE & DESCRIPTION |
|-----|------|--------------------|
| A | 9 | 71-7/8-in. (backer boards, upper shelf legs and rims) |
| B | 4 | 68-7/8-in. (work surface and lower shelf rim) |
| C | 4 | 35-1/2-in. (legs) |
| D | 4 | 27-in. (end rims) |
| E | 5 | 24-in. (work surface joists) |
| F | 5 | 15-in. (lower shelf joists) |
| G | 7 | 9-in. (upper shelf joists) |

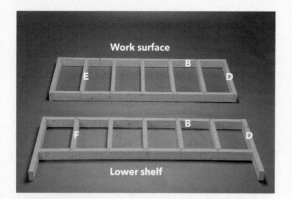

Work surface
E B D

F B D
Lower shelf

**1** Assemble the frames for the work surface and lower shelf

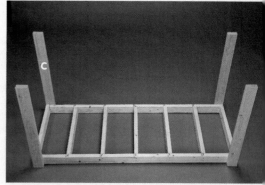

C

**2** Screw the legs onto the frame for the bench's work surface

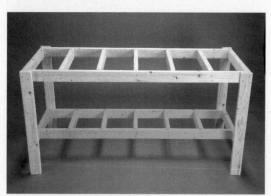

**3** Flip over the bench and attach the lower shelf frame

**4** Screw the plywood to the frames

A G

**5** Assemble the top shelf frame

### TIP
Use paint cans to support the lower shelf frame when you're attaching it to the workbench's main legs.

**6** Add the plywood

## FIGURE C
## 2x4 USAGE
## DIAGRAM

Waste

E

G
F
D

G
G
G
F
G

A A B

C

C

A

**7** Attach the top shelf legs upside down

# Add to It!

### LIGHTING
A bench is only as good as the light it's under. Buy a 4-ft. shop light for less than $15 and screw it to the underside of the top shelf.

### POWER STRIP
Mount a power strip to one of the legs, and use its switch to control the light. It's easy and convenient.

### PEGBOARD
Keep down the bench clutter by stowing all of those tools you use every day within easy reach.

Backer boards

**8** Screw the legs to the bench and add the backer boards

# 11 WAYS TO LOOSEN NUTS, BOLTS & SCREWS

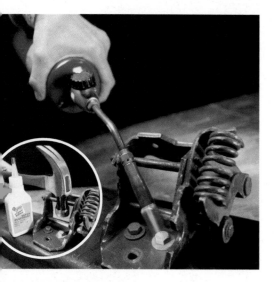

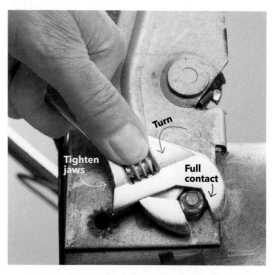

### 1. HEAT TO THE RESCUE

Heat, oil and tapping will unstick most nuts and bolts in metal. Apply only enough heat to cause expansion in the entire bolt–about a minute or so for the average-size bolt. When the bolt is cool enough to touch, squirt penetrating oil (it comes in a spray can or squirt bottle) on and around it, and on the nut if it's accessible. Be careful–that stuff is flammable. Tap the end of the bolt several times with a hammer to help loosen the threads and allow the oil to penetrate. Wait another minute or so for the oil to work, and then use your wrench.

### 2. ADJUSTABLE WRENCH TECHNIQUE

An adjustable wrench isn't the ideal tool for loosening stuck fasteners because it can round over the head, making matters worse. But if an adjustable wrench is your only option, here's your best shot at preserving the shoulders on the nut or bolt head: Slide on the wrench all the way, so there's full contact at the back of the jaws. Then tighten the wrench thumbscrew so there's no play at all in the jaws. Always turn the wrench handle toward the lower jaw, never away from it.

**CAUTION** The cheater bar technique can exceed the design strength of the tool, cause it to break and void the tool warranty. Wear eye protection.

### 3. USE A CHEATER BAR (AND THE RIGHT SOCKET)

Be a cheater by slipping a short length of pipe–a cheater bar –over the end of your tool handle. The extra length gives you much better leverage. Be careful, though, not to use so much force that you break the tool or break the head off the shank of the bolt.

You'll find six-point sockets get a better grip on hex nuts and bolts than 12-point sockets, which are designed to fit both hex and square fasteners.

Flat

New slot

## 4. MANGLED SLOT (SOLUTION 1)

If the slot of a roundhead screw or bolt is chewed up beyond hope of gripping it with a screwdriver, file two flat edges on it. Then turn the head with an adjustable wrench.

## 5. MANGLED SLOT (SOLUTION 2)

Use a hacksaw to cut a new slot at a right angle to the old one. For big screws, put two blades in your hacksaw, right next to each other, and cut a wider slot so you can use a big screwdriver. This is also a great way to get a grip on the head of a stuck carriage bolt, which has no slot or flats.

## 6. OFF WITH ITS HEAD

When there's no other solution— when heat, penetrating oil and wrenches have all failed—use a hacksaw to cut off bolt heads or nuts, (you can also use a cold chisel or a reciprocating saw). Some smaller fasteners, such as rivets and flathead bolts, may be easier to drill out than to cut.

## 7. GET A GRIP

When a bolt head has become so rounded that a wrench won't get a bite, use locking pliers. Get a tight grip: You may have only two or three chances before the head gets so rounded that even this won't work. Use penetrating oil, heat and tapping if it slips after your first try.

## 8. STICKING SCREW

Try a wrench on a screwdriver blade for a big screw that just won't budge. Select the largest screwdriver that'll fit, and tap the butt of the handle with a hammer. Lean your weight onto the screwdriver to keep it in the slot as you turn it with your wrench. Too much torque bends the screwdriver tip—be careful!

## . SPLIT A NUT

 nut splitter, also called a nut
racker, will crack any no-turn
ut without damaging the bolt
hreads or stem that it's screwed
nto. Just slip the ring over the
ut and turn the tooth into it
ntil it breaks. You can find a nut
racker at Sears, Amazon and
ther tool stores.

## 0. A SCREW EXTRACTOR

 screw extractor could save your day. It will grab
bout any threaded fastener and remove it—even
 the head has snapped off. It usually comes with
 hardened drill bit to drill a hole in the center of
our stubborn screw or bolt. Then you turn the
xtractor counterclockwise into the hole. A tapered
hape and left-handed thread make it possible for
he extractor to jam in the hole and then begin to
urn out the screw.

## 11. IMPACT DRIVER

An impact driver works with a bladed or Phillips
head screwdriver bit, or a socket head. Striking
the tool does three things at once: The blow
loosens the thread bond; the downward force
keeps the tool in the slot; and the head of the tool
turns 20 degrees in the loosening direction. Make
sure the screw slot is clean and free of debris.

# CHAPTER 5

EASY FIXES

## A BETTER WAY TO CLEAN CAST-IRON

Removing baked-on food from a cast-iron pan is tricky. Soap can strip away the pan's seasoning, so what do you do? Scrunch up a piece of tinfoil and run hot water over the pan, using the foil to scour away the stuck-on food.

## STAY ON THE PAGE

Keeping a cookbook open as you're making your meal can be difficult. Solve the problem with something you have in your kitchen: a chip clamp. Use it to hold open the pages (and next time you're at the grocery store, pick up a couple of extras to use just for this purpose!).

# Stay-Put Trash Bag

Don't you hate it when the plastic bag in your garbage can slips down inside as it fills up? Solve the problem easily with drawstring garbage bags and an adhesive-backed hook. Stick the hook on the back of the trash can a few inches below the top. As the bag gets heavier, the drawstring gets taut and pulls the top of the plastic bag tighter against the bin so it doesn't slip inside!

# Slip-Free Drink Holders

It's always nice to relax and sip a cold one in your Adirondack chair, but if you set your drink down, small movements could send it sliding off the edge. To solve the problem, drill a hole in the arm of the chair with a 3-in. hole saw. Take two short lengths of heavy-duty strapping (available at camping stores), cross them at the bottom and use two-part epoxy glue to attach the straps under the arm. Now you can really relax!

## MAKE YOUR OWN HEATING PAD

Next time you have a sore neck or aching back, don't reach for an electric heating pad. Instead, fill a sock with uncooked rice, tie the end and microwave it for two or three minutes. It works far better than a heating pad because it conforms to your body. You can even add some cinnamon or lavender to make it smell nice!

## BOTTLE GNAT TRAP

Want to get rid of gnats or fruit flies? Wash a soda bottle, cut off the top and make a line at the one-third mark. Dissolve 3 Tbsp. of sugar in 1/4 cup of vinegar, pour it in and add water up to the line. Set the top upside down in the bottle. The pests can easily get in, but it's hard for them to get out. Place the trap wherever those insects gather, and they'll soon be gone.

## EASY LABEL REMOVAL

Old plastic containers are very useful for storing parts and fasteners, but getting the old label off can be tough. If you fill the container with hot water, the label will peel right off after a few minutes. If your tap water is hot enough, fill the container, wait for the adhesive to soften and then peel the label. If you heat the water on the stove, don't boil it! Keep the water at about 160 degrees F—if it gets too much higher, your container can sag and lose its shape.

## FRESH, CLEAN CUTTING BOARD

Here's an easy and effective way to get stains out of your cutting boards: Sprinkle coarse salt over the surface and scrub with half a lemon. Then just rinse and dry.

# Less-Mess Food Funnel

Avoid spilling food after chopping by funneling it through the handle of the cutting board into the bowl. Just set the handle hole over the bowl and scrape the food into the hole.

# Defuzz Your Roller

New roller covers have lint on them that will end up on your wall when you start to paint. To avoid this, roll the cover over a strip of tape before painting.

## JUST-IN-CASE CASH

These days, you're much more likely to forget your wallet at home than you are your phone. Keep a little extra cash tucked behind your phone case for emergencies.

## HANDS-FREE DOOR TRICK

Need to go in and out of the same door a bunch of times while carrying stuff? To keep the door from latching shut, loop a rubber band around one doorknob or handle, and then twist it once and loop it around the other knob. The rubber band holds the latch in. Now if the door closes, you can push it open with your body whenever your hands are full.

## GLOW-IN-THE-DARK LAMP SWITCH

It can be hard to see pull chains on fluorescent lamp fixtures in the basement, and if it's around the corner from the doorway, it's even worse! To make the chain easier to find in the dim light, drill a hole in the middle of a glow-in-the-dark ball and tie it onto the pull switch. You'll have no trouble finding it now.

## NEVER FORGET THE COMBINATION

If you struggle to remember your lock combination, try this: Pick a secret number and add it to each of your combination's numbers. Mark your resulting higher numbers on the lock itself with a marker or rotary tool. When you need to open the lock, subtract your number from each number to determine the correct combination.

## Draft Dodger

If your home has round ceiling registers for the air-conditioning system, in winter, you might get cold air falling from the registers. Rather than put up with the cool drafts, seal those registers with clear plastic saucers that you put under flowerpots. Temporarily glue them in place with White Lightning SEASONSeal Clear Removable Weather Stripping ($5). It's a rubbery sealant that you apply with a caulk gun and peel off in the spring.

# Garbage Lid Hinge

Are you tired of losing your garbage can lid? Attach it to the barrel with cable ties. Drill 1/4-in. holes for your ties, and then double them for extra strength. The lid will flip open and stay connected to the barrel. Best of all, you'll never have to search for your lid again!

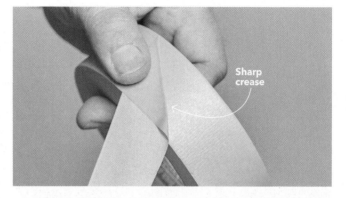

Sharp crease

# TAPE-TEARING TIP

Here's an easy way to tear your tape and get a starting edge at the same time. Simply fold the tape under at a 90-degree angle to the roll. Then, with a snapping motion, pull the tape against the edge of the roll. The tape tears, leaving a triangular starting tab. This won't work with plastic tapes; those must be cut.

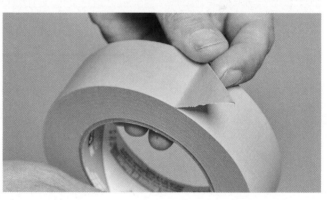

## ADJUSTABLE TABLE HEIGHT

It's often useful to have a laptop close by when you work on projects so you can refer to an article or take notes. Craft tables are often too low for comfort by themselves, so get some pieces of 1-1/4-in. PVC pipe to slip over the legs. Measure the height so it's just right—no more aching back! The pipe pieces are easy to slip off.

# No-Slide Kneepads

Kneepads that slip down your shins every time you stand up are a huge nuisance. Avoid the slide by strapping on a pair of hockey or baseball catchers' shinguards instead. You get comfortable kneepads that stay put, and shin protection, too. You can try a secondhand sports store or get a new pair for about $30 online.

# Pet Repellent for Furniture

To train your pets to stay off the furniture, place plastic carpet protectors—prickly side up—on their favorite perch. Available in office supply stores and the carpet/flooring department in most home centers, these protectors can be cut to the size you need with a scissors or a utility knife. The plastic teeth will train your pets to associate the couch with being uncomfortable. Soon they will seek cozier spots to relax on and leave the easy chair to you. Just remember to remove the protector for your derriere.

# DOG-SPOT SOLUTIONS

Growing a neat lawn in an area frequented by dogs is difficult, but not impossible. Acidic dog urine discolors and kills the grass, leaving a nasty patchwork of noticeable brown spots. Here are a few tricks for keeping the grass green:

1. Apply lime or gypsum regularly to neutralize the acid in the soil and restore the balance that grass prefers.
2. Water the area heavily each week to dilute the urine.
3. Don't fight it! Replace the grass with small round gravel (pea rock) bordered with stone cobbles or brick. Place some landscape fabric beneath the rock to prevent weeds from popping up and your problem is solved, permanently. Another plus—you'll have less grass to mow!

## A BETTER LITTER BOX

To keep your cat's litter in the box where it belongs, mark an opening on one end of a large plastic storage container, then push a sharp razor knife into the plastic and cut out the opening. Pour in the litter and your cat will figure out the rest.

## CHEW-FREE ELECTRICAL CORDS

Some dogs just love gnawing on electrical cords around the house. This is quite dangerous, and really irritating when they destroy computer cables. Solve the problem by wrapping the cords with split flexible plastic conduit that you get at home centers and automotive stores. Just cut the length you need and push the cords into the presplit slot. Dogs will completely lose interest in the cords. Your next challenge: Get them to stop chewing up your slippers!

# Easier Bath Time

For a calmer and easier bath time, make a dog-washing station in your shower. Cover the drain with a hair catcher to prevent fur from clogging it. Cut a hole in a bath mat so it fits over the drain and lay it in the shower to prevent your dog from slipping around. Temporarily replacing your showerhead with a hand-held sprayer gives you more control and lets you avoid spraying water into your pet's ears. Dogs like the extra space in the shower, you don't have to reach awkwardly over the tub, and everyone involved will find bath day a whole lot more pleasant.

## Outdoor Doggy Doo-Doo Holder

If you're a dog owner, getting rid of all those little bags of doggy doo-doo, especially in winter, can be a pain. They get lost in the snow if you put them outside, and if you toss them directly into your outdoor garbage can, they fall to the bottom and get stuck until spring (yuck!). Use an old mailbox mounted on a post as your doo-doo collector. Stick a shopping bag inside, toss in the little collection bags all week long, and then tie up the larger bag and toss it in the garbage can.

## LEASH SAVER

When you have a puppy or a dog that chews on its leash, protect the leash with 3/4-in. vinyl hose. Cut the hose into 3-in. pieces and thread them onto the leash until you reach the end. Cutting the vinyl into pieces makes it slide more easily over the leash and also keeps the leash pliable.

## ELEVATED DOG DISH

Some larger dogs can have difficulty eating from dishes on the floor. To give your dog a break, cut a plastic pail in half and then glue the dog food dish to the bottom of it with adhesive caulk. Your dog just might be even more enthusiastic than ever about eating.

# CORD CLIP

A paper binder clip works great to manage small electrical cords. Use one to keep long headphone cords neatly wound and tangle-free.

# Save Your Wet Cellphone (It's Worth a Shot)

If you act fast, there's a chance you can save your wet cellphone. First, *don't* turn it on. You'll short it out, and that'll be it for the phone. Instead, immediately remove the battery (and the SIM card, if you have one) and use a clean cloth to dry off the phone inside and out. Don't use a hair dryer or anything else hot to dry it; you'll damage the components. To absorb any leftover moisture, put the battery and phone in an airtight container filled with uncooked rice, close the lid, and let it sit overnight. The next morning, insert the battery, cross your fingers and power it up. You might be pleasantly surprised, and if it doesn't work, at least you tried.

# New Laptop Foot

While typing on a laptop's keyboard, you might notice that it rocks slightly. Check out the bottom—one of the hard rubber feet could be missing. This doesn't have to be an expensive repair, though; grab your caulk gun and a tube of black silicone and squeeze out a small amount on the missing foot. Level the caulk with a toothpick and let it set overnight. The next day the silicone will be hard and should work perfectly.

# Enlarge Tiny Print

The print on some containers is so small that even someone with perfect vision would have some trouble reading it. Instead of searching for a magnifying glass, grab your phone and snap a photo of the text. Now, you can open the photo and zoom in to make the words legible.

## A DAB MARKS THE TOP

Tired of guessing which side of a USB plug should face up when you're plugging it into the port? Put a dab of hot glue on the top face of the plug. Now you'll be able to tell the right direction without even looking.

# INSTANT PHONE STAND

Need to prop up your phone to watch a video or look at project plans? A couple of zip ties are all you need. Secure one zip tie around each end of your phone, using the excess "tail" to keep the phone upright.

## Poster-Putty Port Cleaner

If you use your computer in the shop, the magnetic charging port can collect a bunch of metal filings and sawdust. Solve the problem with a ball of poster putty. It removes debris without leaving any residue.

# Reinforce Your Phone Cord

Phone cords tend to wear out where the cord enters the plug end. To reinforce your cords, slide a bit of heat-shrink tubing over the weak spot. Hold the cord with pliers and wave a lighter under the tubing. The tubing shrinks around the cord and plug end, making the junction more durable.

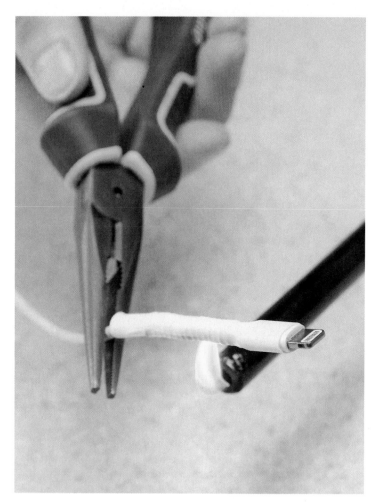

## SEAT-GAP FILLER

Tired of dropping loose change, food and other stuff between your car's seat and the center console? Cut a piece of foam pipe insulation and stick it into the gap.

## LUGGAGE RACK PROTECTOR

Carrying items like ladders on your luggage rack carries the risk of scratching the rack. To keep it scratch-free, cover the bars with pool noodles. Just slit them down the side with a utility knife and tape them on. The cushion of foam keeps some items from rattling, too. Don't forget to strap down your cargo before you go!

WERNER

# Ice-Proof Car Windows

Does your area have heavy frost warnings tonight? Fill a spray bottle with three parts vinegar and one part water. Right before it gets dark outside, shake the mixture well and spray it evenly on your car windows. The acetic acid in the vinegar will prevent water from freezing on your windows overnight.

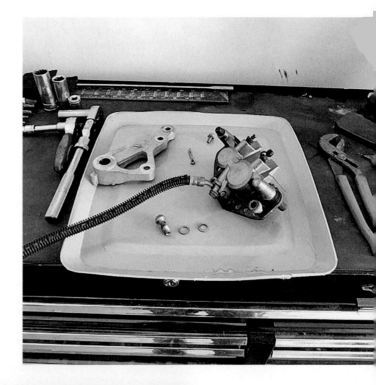

## Laundry Basket Drip Pan

Here's a clever use for broken laundry baskets. Cut off the bottom with a razor knife to make an easy-to-clean drip pan for catching oil drips under your car or keeping greasy parts from wrecking your workbench. It's a simple way to reuse something you'd normally just throw away.

## Instant Oil Funnel

Don't have a funnel handy? An empty plastic oil container will do the job. Cut the bottom out of the empty container with a utility knife. This funnel can hold an oil container snugly, so you don't have to stand around and wait for the last drop to drain.

# DIY FLOOR MATS

Want to keep your car's original mats free of road salt and mud? Cut a few carpet scraps to fit on the floor. We found these carpet samples for less than $2 each at Home Depot. When the carpet scraps get dirty, you can take them out and hose them off. Caution: For the driver's side, be sure to punch holes in the corners of the carpet and lash it to the seat rails. This prevents it from sliding forward and interfering with the pedals.

## NO-SLIDE CARGO

Here's a great idea for keeping grocery bags, tools and other equipment from shifting around in the back of your pickup or SUV. Use an adjustable shower curtain rod to keep everything in place. You can move it around to wherever you need it, and it keeps everything right where you put it.

# Fix for a Slippery Situation

Tired of your GPS sliding off the dashboard every time you take a corner a little too fast? You could use a sandbag mount, but it can lose its grip over time. Instead, use a piece of rubbery drawer liner like the kind you put in toolboxes and kitchen drawers. Now that GPS will stay put no matter how crazy your driving gets.

## Squeak-Proof Wipers

Are squeaky windshield wipers driving you crazy? Solve the problem by rubbing your wiper blades with vinegar. It'll prevent streaking and silence your blades, at least for a while.

# LIFT-GATE PROTECTION

When you open the lift gate of your van or SUV, it's easy to hit a cross brace of the garage door and chip the paint on the gate. Protect it by using a pool noodle as a cushion. Just slit the swim noodle with a utility knife and slip it over the brace. You can also use preslit foam pipe insulation. If it slips off, use double-sided tape to hold it in place.

# ULTIMATE
# CONTAINER STORAGE

## TOOLS AND MATERIALS

Our 24-in. base cabinet required a 4 x 4-ft. sheet of 1/2-in.-thick plywood for the rollout, plus a 2 x 3-ft. scrap of 3/4-in. plywood for the carrier. Yours may require more or less. We found some high-quality birch plywood at a home center for this project. If you can't find good plywood, consider ordering Baltic birch or other hardwood plywood from a home center or lumberyard. The carrier fits under the rollout and isn't very conspicuous, so almost any flat piece of 3/4-in. plywood will work for that.

In addition to the lumber, you'll require a pair of 22-in. full-extension ball-bearing slides (about $22 at home centers or woodworking supply stores) and a 1/4-in. aluminum rod.

We used a table saw to cut the plywood parts, but if you're careful to make accurate cuts, a circular saw will work. You'll need a jigsaw with a plywood-cutting blade to cut the curves on the sides and dividers. We used a finish nail gun and 1-1/4-in.-long brad nails to connect the parts, but you could substitute trim-head screws if you don't mind the larger holes they leave.

## MEASURE THE BASE CABINET

Base cabinets are usually about 23 in. deep and accommodate this rollout, but measure yours

Opening width

**1** Measure from any protruding hinges or door parts to the opposite side to find the opening width. Also check to make sure the cabinet is at least 22 in. deep.

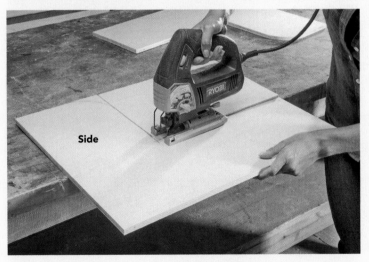

Side

**2** Cut each panel to size. Then cut the notch to form the L-shape. Start with a table saw or circular saw for the straight cuts. Finish the inside corner with a jigsaw.

**3** Mark the curves on the side panels by tracing along a gallon paint can. Mark the dividers using a quart-size paint can. Then cut with a jigsaw.

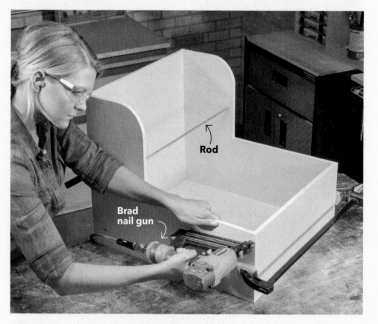

Rod

Brad nail gun

**4** Glue and clamp the parts together. Don't forget to install the rod. Align the edges by tapping on the panels with your hand or a hammer. Then nail the parts together.

to be sure. If the measurement from the back of the face frame to the back of the cabinet is less than 22 in., you'll have to build a shallower rollout and use shorter drawer slides.

Another critical measurement is the width. Measure the clear opening width; that is, the width from any protruding hinge or door parts to the opposite side of the cabinet opening (**Photo 1**). Subtract 3 in. from this measurement to determine the width of parts B, C, D and E.

**CUT OUT THE PARTS**

After adjusting the size of parts B, C, D and E for the cabinet width, you can cut out all the parts except the carrier bottom. If you're using a table saw, make partial cuts to form the L-shaped sides. But remember, you can't see how far the blade is cutting on the underside, so be sure to stop short of your inside corner marks by at least an inch. **Photo 2** shows how to complete the cut with a jigsaw.

Trace along the edge of a 1-gallon paint can to draw the radius for the curve on the side panels. Trace along a quart-size can to draw the radius on the dividers. Cut the curves on the sides and dividers with a jigsaw (**Photo 3**). Smooth the curved cuts with 100-grit sandpaper.

**BUILD THE ROLLOUT**

Mark the location of the 1/4-in. rod on the side panels using Figure A as a guide. Wrap tape around a 1/4-in. drill bit 1/4 in. from the end to use as a depth guide while drilling.

Drill 1/4-in.-deep holes at the marks, and then use a hacksaw o cut an aluminum rod 1/2 in. onger than the width of he bottom.

Apply wood glue to all edges hat meet, and then arrange the sides, bottom, front and back on a workbench and clamp them together. Work the rod into the holes. Tap the parts with a hammer to align the edges perfectly before connecting them with brad nails (**Photo 4**). Take your time aiming the nail gun to avoid nail blowouts.

Finish the rollout by adding the dividers. First decide how many dividers you want and calculate the width of the space between the dividers. Cut a spacer block to that dimension and use it as a guide to install the dividers. Attach the dividers to the shelf (**Photo 5**). Then measure down 7-1/2 in. from the top and make marks to indicate the top edge of the divider shelf. Line up the divider assembly with these marks and nail it in. Draw divider center lines on the back of the rollout as a nailing guide. Then attach the dividers (**Photo 6**).

Drawer slides require 1/2-in. clearance on each side. Making the carrier exactly 1 in. wider than the rollout will result in a perfect fit. Measure the width of the completed rollout and add exactly 1 in. to determine the width of the carrier bottom.

Cut the carrier bottom from 3/4-in. plywood. Then screw the carrier sides to the carrier bottom to prepare it for mounting the drawer slides.

## MOUNT THE SLIDES

Follow the instructions included with your slides to separate the

### CUTTING LIST

| KEY | QTY. | MATERIAL | DIMENSIONS | PART |
|-----|------|----------|------------|------|
| A | 2 | 1/2-in. plywood | 1/2 in. x 22 in. x 18 in. | Sides |
| B | 1 | 1/2-in. plywood | 1/2 in. x 7-1/2 in. x 18 in. | Front |
| C | 1 | 1/2-in. plywood | 1/2 in. x 22 in. x 18 in. | Bottom |
| D | 1 | 1/2-in. plywood | 1/2 in. x 17-1/2 in. x 18 in. | Back |
| E | 1 | 1/2-in. plywood | 1/2 in. x 7-1/2 in. x 18 in. | Shelf |
| F | 5* | 1/2-in. plywood | 1/2 in. x 6 in. x 6 in. | Dividers |
| G | 1 | 3/4-in. plywood | 3/4 in. x 20 in. x 22 in. | Carrier bottom |
| H | 2 | 3/4-in. plywood | 3/4 in. x 2-3/4 in. x 22 in. | Carrier sides |

**Note:** These sizes are for a 24-in.-wide base cabinet. To fit your cabinet, adjust the sizes according to the instructions in the article.

**5** Cut a spacer the width of the desired space between dividers and use it to position the dividers as you nail them to the shelf.

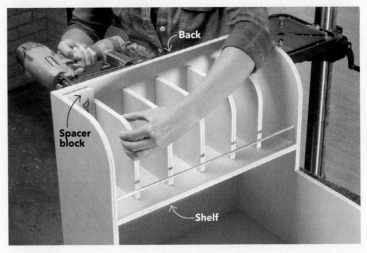

**6** Position the shelf and nail through the sides into the shelf. Use the spacer block to align dividers and nail through the back.

## MATERIALS LIST

| ITEM | QTY. |
| --- | --- |
| 1/2" x 4' x 4' plywood | 1 |
| 3/4" x 2' x 3' plywood | 1 |
| Pair of 22" full-extension slides | 1 |
| 36" x 1/4" aluminum rod | 1 |
| Small package of 1-1/4" brad nails | 1 |

slides into two parts: a channel and a rail. Usually, pressing down on a plastic lever releases the parts and allows you to separate them. Screw the rails to the drawer (**Photo 7**) and the channels to the carrier sides (**Photo 8**).

When you're done installing the slides, check for the fit by carefully aligning the rails with the channels and sliding them together. The rollout should glide easily on the ball-bearing slides. If the slides seem too tight, you can adjust the fit by removing one of the carrier sides and slipping a thin cardboard shim between the carrier side and carrier bottom before reassembling them.

## MOUNT THE ROLLOUT IN THE CABINET

**Photo 9** shows fitting the carrier assembly into the cabinet. It will have a little side-to-side play, so you can adjust the position to clear the hinge and door. This will probably require you to offset the carrier slightly away from the hinge side.

Screw the carrier to the bottom of the cabinet and you're ready to install the rollout (**Photo 10**). Since you've checked the fit, it should operate perfectly. Now load it up with containers and lids and enjoy your new neatly organized container rollout.

**FIGURE A**

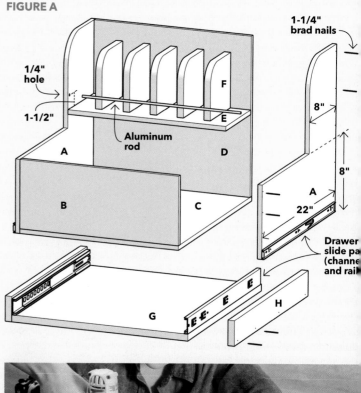

**7** Separate the drawer slides and attach the rail to the rollout. Align the rail flush to the bottom and flush to the front before driving the screws.

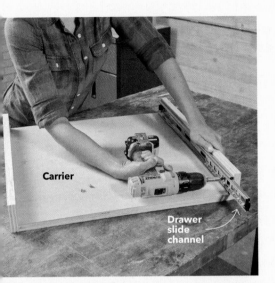

Carrier

Drawer
slide
channel

**8** Rest the drawer slide channel on the carrier and align the front flush to the front of the carrier side.

**9** Position the carrier so that the rollout will clear any hinge or door parts. Drive screws through the carrier bottom into the cabinet.

**10** Line up the rails and channels and slide the rollout into the cabinet. Slide it back and forth a few times to make sure it rolls smoothly.

# FIX A LEAKY TOILET

### Stop seeing water where it shouldn't be with these flange fixes.

**IF YOUR TOILET LEAKS** around the base, there's a problem with the toilet-to-flange connection. It may be as simple as a wax ring that needs to be replaced. It's important to stop leaks as soon as possible; even minor ones can cause substantial damage over time (and cost you money, too). Here are the most common problems you'll find under the toilet and how to address them.

**MEET THE EXPERT**
**Les Zell has been a plumber for almost 30 years and an invaluable resource to** *Family Handyman* **for the past decade. He's the owner/operator of Zell Plumbing & Heating.**

# Flange Fix-It Options

Broken flange

Repair bracket

## TWO-PART REPAIR RING

Steel flanges that surround plastic flanges can rust away. A simple solution is to install a two-part (or hinged) ring ($15) that locks under the plastic rim. Badly corroded steel rings can be pried and peeled away. If you have to get aggressive, cut it away with an angle grinder or oscillating tool fitted with a metal-cutting blade.

## EARED REINFORCEMENT RING

If you have just a small amount of rot surrounding the flange, or screws won't be able to grip the wood under a repair flange, you might get away with an eared reinforcement ring. The ears may extend beyond the rot enough to get a good grip in the subfloor for the screws. Use six 1-1/2-in. No. 8 oval-head stainless steel screws to anchor it in wood. If you have concrete, use 1-1/4-in. flat-head concrete screws.

Ear

Broken flange

## REPAIR BRACKETS

Cast-iron flanges often break on one or both sides. If only the bolt slot is damaged, slip a repair bracket ($5) under the cast-iron lip. It will be held in place by the unbroken cast-iron lip and provide a new slot for the flange bolt.

Broken flange

Repair flange

## REPAIR RING

Plastic flanges often bend or break, but here's an easy fix. Just screw a stainless steel repair ring ($6) over the plastic flange with at least four 1-1/2-in. stainless steel screws. Consider doing this even if you find that the flange is in good shape and you only need to replace the wax ring. It's cheap insurance against trouble. The repair ring raises the flange about 1/4 in., so before you install the ring, test it over the flange and then see if the toilet rocks when you set it on top. If it does, you'll need to shim under the toilet to allow for the extra height.

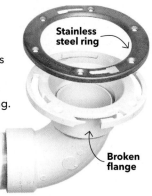

Stainless steel ring

Broken flange

## REPAIR FLANGE

If the flange is in bad shape, you can install a plastic flange ($25) that slips inside (shown above). Home centers carry versions of these. Or you can add a brass ring ($7) similar to a stainless steel ring. If necessary, break away the cast-iron flange with a cold chisel.

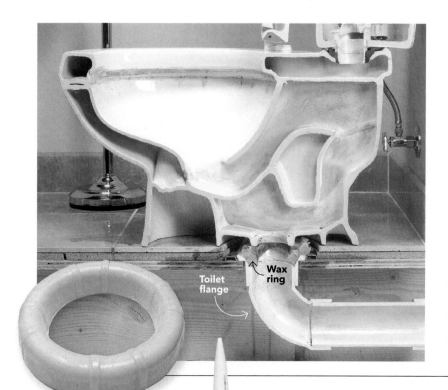

Toilet
flange

Wax
ring

## HOW A WAX RING WORKS

A wax ring is the most commonly used seal between the toilet and the toilet flange. There are synthetic versions, but traditional wax rings (made from beeswax) are the go-to choice for most plumbers—the pros and amateurs alike.

When the toilet is set, the wax is compressed and reshaped to form a watertight seal. Because the wax doesn't harden or degrade, the seal will last for a very long time if the toilet is set properly and firmly bolted down.

## BUY EVERY FLANGE FIX SOLD!

You never know what you're going to find when you pull the toilet, so you have to be prepared so you can get your toilet working again fast. You can always return the items you don't use. (Don't buy the cast-iron repair parts unless you have cast-iron drain lines.) In addition to the flange fixes, get two wax rings, a new set of brass toilet flange bolts, plastic toilet shims and a tube of tub/tile caulk.

Toilet shim

## DON'T IGNORE A ROCKING TOILET!

If your toilet is rocking or wobbling, don't ignore it, even if it's not leaking. Eventually the wax ring or toilet base seal will fail and you'll have a leak. Shim under the toilet with plastic toilet shims until it's steady. Trim the shims and snug up the flange nuts. Then caulk around the base of the toilet with tub/tile caulk.

Stainless steel rim

## CHOOSE FLANGES WITH STAINLESS STEEL RIMS

If you have access under the toilet, replacing a bad or corroded flange is sometimes the best and easiest solution. Because all plastic flanges are prone to breakage, and plastic flanges with ordinary steel rims are prone to rotting away, the best choice is a plastic flange surrounded with stainless steel. Go downstairs and investigate. Depending on access, you may need elbows, more pipe and a coupling to tie in the new one.

# Dealing With Floor Rot

If your toilet has been leaking for some time, you're likely to have rot. The rot can range from a little bit to a case that requires replacing subflooring and possibly framing.

Flange support bracket

## MODERATE ROT

If the rot extends beyond the range of an eared flange but is still contained within the footprint of the toilet, step up to a flange support bracket ($20). These brackets transfer the load past the rotted areas of the subfloor.

New wood

## EXTENSIVE ROT

Don't freak out if you have bad floor rot. It's easier than you think to cut out the bad flooring and replace it with new wood and additional framing if needed. Just make sure you go far enough to cover the entire area of rotted wood. Bad framing can usually be left in place and reinforced with new 2-by material, if you can screw it into solid wood. Don't worry about removing the rotted framing. With the leak fixed, the rot won't continue. The worst part is that you'll also need to replace the finished floor.